Mischief, Caprice
and Other Poetic Strategies

MISCHIEF, CAPRICE

and Other Poetic Strategies

an anthology of poems
based on twenty little poetry projects

edited by Terry Wolverton

Red Hen Press 🐓 Los Angeles

MISCHIEF, CAPRICE, AND OTHER POETIC STRATEGIES

Book design by Mark E. Cull
Colver design by Susan Silton, S∅S Los Angeles

ISBN 1-888996-17-X
Library of Congress Catalog Card Number 2004095948

The City of Los Angeles Cultural Affairs Department, California Arts Council and the Los Angeles County Arts Commision partially support Red Hen Press.

First Edition

Red Hen Press
www.redhen.org

Acknowledgments

"Moon, Go Away, I Don't Love You No More," by Jim Simmerman was first published in *Poetry*, and reprinted in *The Practice of Poetry*, HarperCollins: New York, NY, 1991. © Jim Simmerman, 1991. Permission of HarperCollins.

"Another Celestial Circuit in North Florida" by Wendy Bishop was first published in *The Ohio Poetry Review*, Spring/Summer 1995: 19–21. © Wendy Bishop, 1995. Permission of author.

"Untitled #4" by Patricia Carlin was first published in *Original Green*, Marsh Hawk Press: East Rockaway, NY, 2003. © Patricia Carlin, 2003. Permission of author.

"untitled (Love's a bird)" by Catherine Daly was first published in *Locket*, Tupelo Press: Dorset, VT, 2004. © Catherine Daly, 2004. Permission of author.

"Stitching Up the Past" by Dina Hardy was first published in *So Luminous the Wildflowers: An Anthology of California Poets*, Tebot Bach: Huntington Beach, CA, 2003. © Dina Hardy, 2003. Permission of author.

"Pentecost" by Michael Hoerman was first published in *Bad Rotten*, Pudding House Publications: Columbus, OH, 2004. © Michael Hoerman, 2004. Permission of author.

"The Opposite of Seeds" by Robin Jacobson was first published in *Mudlark: an electronic journal of poetry & poetics*: Spring 2004. © Robin Jacobson, 2004. Permission of author.

"Deceitful Beyond All Cure" by Rhoda Janzen was first published in *Buffalo Carp*: Fall 2002. © Rhoda Janzen, 2002. Permission of author.

"*Felis Rufus*" by Diane Lockward was first published in *Eve's Red Dress*, Wind Publications: Nicholasville, KY, 2003. © Diane Lockward, 2003. Permission of author.

"We Dream of Heroes" by Frances Ruhlen McConnel was first published in *Mudlark: an electric journal of poetry & poetics*, November 2001. © Frances Ruhlen McConnel, 2001. Permission of author.

"Masculinity in Springtime" by Jeff Mock was first published in *Sundog: The Southwest Review*, vol. 20, no. 20: Fall 2000. © Jeff Mock, 2000. Permission of author.

"The Death of Soul" by Renee Simms was first published in a slightly different version in *Inkwell Journal*: Purchase, NY, 2003. © Renee Simms, 2003. Permission of author.

"Poem to Beer" by David Starkey was first published in *Open City*, no. 12, 2001. © David Starkey, 2001. Permission of author.

"Every Dog's Martini" by Lynne Thompson was first published in *We Arrive by Accumulation*, SeaMoon Press: Sedona, AZ, 2002. © Lynne Thompson 2002. Permission of author.

"High Performance, Low Mileage," by William Trowbridge was first published in *ACM (Another Chicago Magazine)*. Permission of author.

The editor wishes to thank the following for their generous contributions to the publication of this book: Dylan Gailey, Sondra Hale, Matt Knight, Susan Silton, all other donors, and the Amgen Foundation.

Contents

Twenty Little Poetry Projects

1. Begin the poem with a metaphor.
2. Say something specific but utterly preposterous.
3. Use at least one image for each of the five senses, either in succession or scattered randomly throughout the poem.
4. Use one example of synesthesia (mixing the senses.)
5. Use the proper name of a person and the proper name of a place.
6. Contradict something you said earlier in the poem.
7. Change direction or digress from the last thing you said.
8. Use a word (slang?) you've never seen in a poem.
9. Use an example of false cause-effect logic.
10. Use a piece of "talk" you've actually heard (preferably in dialect and/or which you don't understand).
11. Create a metaphor using the following construction: The (adjective) (concrete noun) of (abstract noun)…"
12. Use an image in such a way as to reverse its usual associative qualities.
13. Make the persona or character in the poem do something he/she could not do in "real life."
14. Refer to yourself by nickname and in the third person.
15. Write in the future tense, such that part of the poems seems to be a prediction.
16. Modify a noun with an unlikely adjective.
17. Make a declarative assertion that sounds convincing but that finally makes no sense.
18. Use a phrase from a language other than English.
19. Make a nonhuman object say or do something human (personification).
20. Close the poem with a vivid image that makes no statement but that "echoes" an image from earlier in the poem.

Open the poem with the first project and close it with the last. Otherwise, use the projects in whatever order you like, giving each project at least one line. Try to use all twenty projects. Feel free to repeat those you like. Fool around. Enjoy.

JIM SIMMERMAN

Moon Go Away, I Don't Love You No More

1. Morning comes on like a wink in the dark.
2. It's me it's winking at.
3. Mock light lolls in the boughs of the pines.
   Dead air numbs my hands.
   A bluejay jabbers like nobody's business.
   Woodsmoke comes spelunking my nostrils
   and tastes like burned toast where it rests on my tongue.
4. Morning tastes the way a rock felt
   kissing me on the eye:
5. a kiss thrown by Randy Shellhouse
   on the Jacksonville, Arkansas Little League field
   because we were that bored in 1965.
6. We weren't *that* bored in 1965.
7. Dogs ran amuck in the yards of the poor,
   and music spilled out of every window
   though none of us could dance.
8. None of us could do the Frug, the Dirty Dog
9. because we were small and wore small hats.
10. *Moon go away, I don't love you no more*
    was the only song we knew by heart.
11. The dull crayons of sex and meanness
    scribbled all over our thoughts.
12. We were about as happy as headstones.
13. We fell through the sidewalk
    and changed color at night.
14. Little Darry was there to scuff through it all,
15. so that today, tomorrow, the day after that
    he will walk backward among the orphaned trees
16. and toy rocks that lead him
    nowhere I could ever track,
    till he's so far away, so lost
17. I'll have to forget him to know where he's gone.
18. *la grave poullet du soir est toujours avec moi—*
19. even as the sky opens for business,
    even as shadows kick off their shoes,
20. even as this torrent of clean morning light
    comes flooding down and over it all.

INTRODUCTION

1. Twenty Projects
Compiling an anthology of poems
can be like drooling before a vast buffet.
The sheer weight of choice may bedazzle or benumb:
salmon so slick pink under the lights,
stench of sterno warming the stroganoff,
jiggling Jell-O jewels in strawberry, lemon, grape.
Hunger nearly drowned by the clatter of voices,
clink of silver from voracious diners.

But what of an anthology of works
all based on the same form? Does that grow tedious
as might, say, fondue
or All-You-Can-Eat Shrimp Night
at Red Lobster in Torrance, California?
When the "form" derives from Jim Simmerman's
"Twenty Little Poetry Projects," the answer
is a resounding "no." All manner of unanticipated
delights appear on the groaning table; mounds
of Sevruga caviar jostle for space with neon
orange Cheetos, only to be overshadowed
by succulent slices of guava. One hungers
to taste it all, and each morsel merely deepens
the craving for culinary excess.

And what of the anthologist? Though she may
fancy herself a judicious *bon vivant* of literature,
perhaps she is only another chowhound
elbowing to the head of the banquet line
because once, the Red Queen told her to run
twice as fast. "I'm too hungry to eat," she pleads
and caresses the magnificent swell of her blubber.
Then she wraps her voluminous flesh in words, syllables
straining their seams to contain her growing appetite.

Precise Puss will record it all, folding the linen
napkins into finicky swans and keeping
the tablecloths ironed. Poetry will be stronger

for being served up in giant ladles and consumed
by gourmands-on-the-go. That final dollop
of persimmon pudding will sing you to sleep
and your dreams will be savory: a literary smorgasbord
where the platters never empty.

2.
Upon receiving my invitation to contribute to *Mischief, Caprice, and Other Poetic Strategies,* celebrated poet Robert Bly penned this letter of response:

> "The whole idea is profoundly stupid, and guaranteed to produce bad
> light verse."

A few other poets of national prominence also demurred, though less emphatically, that an exercise like the "Twenty Little Poetry Projects" just wasn't their cup of tea.

I am grateful to these poets for responding, and I have enormous respect for them and for the necessity for every poet to identify his or her own creative process. Still, I was surprised that any poet might not be at least a little intrigued by the opportunities for adventure offered by the "Twenty Little Poetry Projects."

As a poet, I am always in search of ways to break through my own boundaries, the limits of perception, ideas, autobiography, language. It is the job of a poet, I tell my students, to reveal the world anew, to present what a reader may have looked at a thousand times before but never *seen* or *understood* in this particular way.

As a teacher of poetry I want to help my students to similarly expand their horizons, to loose themselves from the confines of what they think they ought to be doing when they write. The "Twenty Little Poetry Projects" exercise, devised by poet and instructor Jim Simmerman, is a great assist in this endeavor. In *The Practice of Poetry,* edited by Robin Behn and Chase Twitchell, where I first encountered the exercise, Simmerman writes:

> Initially I created this exercise for my beginning poetry writing students who—as best I now
> recall—seemed to me to be overly concerned with transparently logical structures, themes,
> and modes of development at the expense of free-for-all wackiness, inventive play, and the
> sheer oddities of language itself.

One of the delights I have as a teacher is in giving an assignment and then finding the variety of responses to it made by students, the infinite variety of pathways branching out from every germ of conception. This was again illustrated in the responses to the call for submissions to this anthology. Very few poets already had poems based on this exercise sitting in their desks (although a handful actually did!); most created new works based on the exercise, and readers will find both narrative and lyric poems with enormous range of form and content. While I cannot claim that the exercise has induced poets to explore subject matter heretofore unattempted in poetry, I will state that in each case the journey to arrive at the content is unexpected, entertaining, and provocative.

The one hundred poets represented here reside in twenty-seven of our fifty states and the District of Columbia, as well as in Canada, Mexico, and India. Twenty-one are men; the rest, women. One contributor was in the second grade when he wrote his poem (the grandson of another contributor); another is a twelve-year-old girl who was assigned it in a writing workshop.

The potential to engage young people as well as adult poets is one of the charms of the exercise. Contributor Madeline Tiger writes:

> A game is a challenge to a kid (and to some grown-ups, not usually to me). This one looked easy but ultimately felt hard. The best way to "teach" is to get into the work oneself and, by signals, induce the others—a little more honest version of the Tom Sawyer fence gambit. My grandson flopped about under my rapid-fire prompts, but he did (dutifully, perhaps) make up vivid responses; I wrote them down, and we pushed on through Ten Projects (enough for a 2nd grader). In a regular classroom I might change some of prompts to fit the age group and what they know about, but you could use most of these anywhere. It becomes a game of leaps and rejoinders and an exercise in observation. It also frees the child— from rhyme, canonical forms, cliché narrative, etc.

This book has a multitude of intentions: I wanted first to engage poets across the country in an activity they might not have attempted before. Now I wish to share a selection of the results with readers of poetry, teachers and students of poetry, and with working poets. I often turn to the exercise when I have an idea for a poem that I need to kick-start. Even more frequently, I find that one or more of the "projects" will come to me when I feel stuck working on a poem: *Contradict something you said earlier*, I will tell myself, or, *say something that makes no sense*. It works every time.

—Terry Wolverton
Los Angeles, 2004

Mischief, Caprice

and Other Poetic Strategies

Liz Ahl

Moon, Come Back, I Still Love You

The moon has been forgotten like the dead
are forgotten. We buried it in a hole
we dug with our own hands. It powdered our
hands when we bore it down from orbit;
the soft ashen gray of the rabbit. It smelled
like emptiness and let out only one
small sigh of surrender. When we kissed
it goodbye, it left dust in our mouths
and closed its crater eyes. Neil Armstrong was
there for the burial but swears it never
happened. When they went to the moon,
no leggy stew cooed, "In the highly unlikely
event of a water landing, your seat cushion
doubles as a flotation device." Of course,
there would be a water landing; it was highly
likely. As they blasted off, the fuel-packed
rockets of the cold war ate themselves whole,
for brunch. Later, they'd landed on the moon,
about to take the after-dinner stroll
from which they might not return. Walter Cronkite
did a joyful jig on his news desk. Thirty
years from now, sixty years from then, I will
still pine for the moon, still understand it's
a cliché to do so. Persnickety moon, I'm you,
you're me, it's all orbit, but also a kind of twinning—
you and me in the round of it.
Quiero la luna. And moon responds: "Why
am I buried? Why am I dead?" And with my
own old hands, I start digging it out of the earth.

ANGELA BALL

Not About Lummoxes

Today's a caboose from which a ghost hand
Swings a golden lantern. Dogs bark in succession
As if impersonating a set of bells
Played three at a time by a jaunty traveler.
And here are two cardinals endemic
To this region: red and an echo of red.
They must be sleepy as we are
But without the sleep that tags after
Another, better life, before abandonment's cement
Took our footprints. The best way to get mistletoe
Is to shoot it down into a sparsely populated area.
Beware—someone carrying a live tree
May be a tree rustler. If it gets dark enough, we'll sit forever
Watching property gravitate into the hands
Of those who want it most.

Actually, it's not getting dark, but that would have been appetizing
And romantic as a waterfall that has already begun
Backing away.

We're in the Embankment Gardens. My friend Bruce says,
"Park benches experience a lot. If one could talk, what would it say?"
—"'Crikey, Mrs. Marlebone, you've put on weight,'
A Mexican bench, maybe *'¿Porque estas llorando, Chiquita?'* "

To be frank, I'm not an Angie, but I'm an Ang or an Angela: name
Being said all over Italy, in fragrant or sour tones,
To the grocery checker of the white arms,
An art-restorer with slender fingers,
A little girl like a bottle of cherry soda
Who says, "We wish the American Angelas well"
And twirls her sunlit skirt.

PAT BARBER

Drowning

Sudden gust—roaring train on sunset's tracks
carries beaches skyward
melding reds and golds with
blinding sounds of dying light.
Sea scents rising from darkness
spice the bitter taste of loneliness
sliding down his throat
and *Ma'ria* of Cape Hatteras
stirs sand and longing
numbing all senses.

Forget the friggin' woman
the sailor mutters
words muffled because his heart is full
ain't no big deal
living under water, swimming in despair.
His leaky boat of hope
pitched high by rocking surf
an arid sea engulfs him
trapped by nets of soggy reminiscence
pressed hard into his skin
only submerged dreams keep him afloat.
His love, his *Trish*.
Mon dieu. La douleur d'amour.
He shouts above the dying gale
I'll drown in her octopus arms.

Night deepens slowly like dementia
exhausted, he goes below to sleep.
Swaying gently, the bony vessel sighs relief
sea-wind dead as dreams along the strand.

SOLOMON BASS, GRADE 2

The Ferris Wheel

The ferris wheel is a pizza,
tomato sauce splatters all around
I can walk on top of the lake without sinking
My father is cooking shrimp
My mother is practicing violin
Solomon is about to eat the cherry pie
The trees are blowing outside
The rice paper feels rough

I smell the sun coming out
Anna took a plane trip to Japan
The wind stopped blowing and the trees stood still
I play Chocolate Factory with Anna,
then we climb a cacao tree
Yeah, dude!
If you don't nail down the picture, the picture will dance
 "Estapit!"

GRACE BAUER

Lunacy

The moon's a melancholy whore.
She'll go down on
any night that's got a sky,
shining like a fingernail paring
or a silver dime.
You could be living on your own
private island, in a cesspool
or a Circle K, drunk
on stale beer or a fine Chardonnay,
listening to Bach or the Butthole Surfers–
she won't discriminate, caressing
one and all with her cold light.

Once I had a boyfriend named Cowboy.
1974. Philadelphia.
I had yet to hear John Prine's song,
but yes, a free ramblin' man he was.
The moon seemed more precious then.
More authentic, you might say.
My half-Persian, Lola, when not scratching
her fleas or the furniture, was out screwing
every Tomcat in town.
As I recall, the Mummers canceled
New Year's that year, because
the wind would have blown them
from South Street clear up Broad
and into Billy Penn's arms.
And that would have been no one's idea
of a good day, though "Honey, a bad day
depends on your definition of a day."

I can still see the sad sun of hope
breaking through. Our headlights punched out
like stars, punched out like Xmas cookies.
We, ourselves, played like gods
with our fingers. And Honey grew less sweet
by the hour, so we knew, even then, she might
eventually turn bitter about romance
and fling the bauble moon aside
with slippery words she only half believes,
and forget, herself, when she came
to such conclusions.

Oh, *c'est la* fucking *vie* and *que sera!*
The moon's going to tango
all over her eyes anyway,
like a happy woman walking the streets
all day.

ROBIN BECKER

Bi-Polar Pets

The lab, tough judge in a black robe, paces
the border of our yards. Allergic to me
and to spring, she sneezes and barks her way
across the new shoots. She smells my human
wisdom, she tastes my preference for standard
poodles, she hears my steak singing
in the oven and feels my slippered longevity
ticking past her. She sees my fresh outlook,
knows I am as resilient as Louisa May Alcott in Concord,
Massachusetts; my New England self-reliance
attracts her, in spite of herself. She fills the air
with feelings as she sheds, a new habit of the newly
sensitive. Theatrical, she ramps up her shedding
to draw my attention and calls *Hey neighbor, whassup?*
across the yard. Bi-polar canines of Pennsylvania!
If the slick obstacle course of middle age dislodges
your sure footing, get professional help.
Heeding my advice, the lab picks up the phone
and dials her vet. He says, *Tell your neighbor, Rubin
you will make a major contribution to society.*
Thanks to relativism, anyone
can find support nowadays, even crackpot dogs!
I will drive to the petrified mall to escape the pall
cast over the neighborhood, as there will be no tyranny
like that imposed by the maniac-depressive animal kingdom.
Je t'embrasse the lab whispers. (I am as moved as the groundhog
crawling under the crabapple.) Now the underground wires
that pen the lab on her side of the green world begin
to hiss *contraptions, contraptions*, that word
which combines *con* and *trap* and thereby suggests
how gender and history held Louisa May captive
those spring days, when she hurried to the butcher
in Concord, pursued by a French-speaking,
wise-cracking, middle-aged and depressed black dog.

WENDY BISHOP

Another Celestial Circuit in North Florida

I walk out into a dog morning, before leaping flames
of clouds are unleashed, swipe the shooting star down with my free hand,
    hear the owls educate fools with long *hoos,*
    taste humid dew a mile-thick on my forearms,
    smell the froggish night steal away
    look at the tight hat of constellations
    and say a secret name, twice.
I was meant to be another Robert, born in Duluth.
I was never meant to be a fool, hooting morning-long at sleeping owls.
It's night that worries me most: it climbs up my back over low hills
    fitch-like and stealthy.
If I said a fitch was a polecat or weasel, it would be so
    for the time it takes to say
    "But I promised not to be gone anymore weekends."
Those blue weekends of desire.
Who expects to take a cold morning shower?
Like thinking Orion would step down out of the heaven, unbuckle his belt.
Like calling her Ariadne, and asking for help getting out sooner, soonest.
I would expect, the heat of southern mornings could shake up the armadillo in you
    and make you wonder where it is you're going.
Going home, going to a hotel, going all weekend, going to hell,
    the gods and goddesses rearrange themselves in the quilted sky.
"Sleep" is the message. Or was it just "shoot the dog"?
Die sensualische Sprache, has always challenged me.
The dog howls at the humid trees and the trees howl back
    Spanish Moss has girl-fights with humid leaves.
If the fitch can survive this night why so can we.

HANNAH BLEIER

Anahit

Anahit seems a simple tune
hummingbird wings or garage rock
a pure purple taste
seedless as the slivermoon.
She's smiling guilelessly,
her thin forearms twisting like Joshua limbs through cold air.
Cleopatra was no beauty, yet she was Queen of Egypt.
Anahit, not simple, must be Queen of Wheelchairs
Queen of Blindness
Queen of Retardation
to be happy in that chair, that life.
If I understood it, I'd be wise.
"Bebby, Bebby, Bebby!" Anahit's classmate Josef calls all day.
The room smells of paper and dust.
"I hear him call me in my dreams," says Debby, their teacher.
The adorable misnomers of infancy, regrettable by age ten.
So much is expected.
But what if the Salvation Army Santa returned my dollar,
telling me crippled children don't need
my condescending metaphors?
What if he patted my butt like a coach
and said, "Go get 'em, kid. Go find out how
to quit making Anahit a stand-in for your self-pity."
Sport, I'd tell myself (recovering from my surprise)
it's time to get up and walk,
because you can.
I will walk through Death Valley, staring at Joshua trees.
To me they will be
Joshua trees.
Returning to Burbank, I will look at Anahit
and see Anahit.
I will hear her calling classmate and he will seem to me
to be calling.
I will give up metaphors and take up emptiness,
teaching Braille without pity and with a certain
je ne sais quoi.
My Perkins Brailler will type cryptic messages while I sleep.
I won't know whether to interpret them as guidance

or obfuscation, and won't care.
I will merely feel the raised dots when they say,
"Hannah seems a simple tune,"
dot six, dots one-two-five, dot one, dots one-three-four-five
and so on.

LINDA BOSSON

Dust If You Must This Old Gray Bust

The vacuum cleaner dips its nose in dust,
for dust is delectable sprinkled on custard
and soothing when rubbed on the knees.
Its fluffiness is harpists' pizzicato
and Harpo of course is cousin to Karl.
To each according to his need.
The vacuum cleaner is mistaken for
elephants trumpeting the news
that they never forget an anniversary
except for Harpo Marx (Karl's mother)
who whispers to wallpaper wanly:
"You never should have made me
sell my teeth." And mumbles
on the Posturepedic mattress of regret,
as sleep treads on him clumsily
like ballroom dancers in galoshes.
Harpo's appearing on "Oprah" (backward)
sending a message in code
to Betsy the Brillo-haired barmaid
and saying vacuum cleaners reproduce.
"They"ll soon outnumber us," he squeaks.
"Those hateful Hoovers, yes, they'll rule the world."
Researchers have found, he adds,
that the dust in the average Oreck
contains the DNA of fourteen humans
and—*mamma mia!*—a yak.
But suddenly the harp is hiccuping.
The vacuum cleaners of the universe
with far too much dust in their nostrils
are sneezing all over the carpet
quite softly, but in unison.

GAYLE BRANDEIS

Horseradish

I want to be Jewish as horseradish
but other religions keep sticking their tongues in my mouth.
Buddha runs his smooth hand over my thigh, Vashti spoons ambrosia through my lips, Christ waves
frankincense under my nose, Gaia shows me the pink
place between her legs, the Tao whooshes underground like a river,
while Rosh Hoshana apples sing soprano in the distance, waiting for me to dip them
in honey.
The best name I've ever heard, Jewish or not, is Honeysuckle Fishbein; she lived in Hyde Park; my
father loved her.
Actually, he hated her
but he played kick the can in the alley and ate hot peppers wrapped in newspaper.
My grandmother loved gribbinis fried in deep fat.
You only love me because I make a decent matzo ball
so get in my hooptie, bitch;
the warm spud of desire sits in the cupboard, growing pale eyes
while you snarl like noodle pudding,
while you dance Hava Nagila up the wall.
Gayley Whaley says "don't mind the mess"—
we'll all be pulling whiskers out of our teeth,
so fling your placid agnostic sweat my direction, baby.
It won't work until we turn it off.
Semper ubi sub ubi
unless the gravlax in your pocket starts to cough,
unless the horseradish brings a few tears to your eyes.

SUSAN BUIS

Domestic Bliss

Our home was a scorched saucepan.
Every house we left had to be destroyed.
The rooms of a house hold emanations—this one's awash in tears.

In the night our words came to blows, vinegar and vitriol in our mouths.
Next morning the house still smells charred.
He looks across the table at me, his eyes momentarily lucid.
"We're clenched," he says, "we're all so clenched."
I close my eyes; see only vertical bands of light, a high-pitched noise.

My reply is burnt orange sardonic.
"Let's play St. Martha of the housewives, in the house at Galilee—
shall I wash your feet now?"
(Did she do that? or was it her sister Mary?)

Behind the basement bricks white tree roots are pushing.
They create fine hairline cracks in our area pellucida, our eggshell walls.
The bedroom floor is precarious; I can feel my foot go right through it,
arm through the wall.
I can poke my finger into the mouth-pink wall softened with moisture.
"La vie en rose" it ain't.

The broken window of escape lies etched in the crease of my arm.
Scratch my surface with a fingernail, feel the map of seawater ferns.
I am corroded with domestic pleasures.
"You bring it on yourself," he says.
His declarations pin me to the wall.

In stroking moments he called her "buckskin," an animal skin
brown with smoke and brains.
(She will leave this skin behind when she claws her way out.)
can't scrape it out, ruined, ringed in black.

PAMELA BURKE

2:37 p.m. Outside Thompson Middle School – 9/11/01

The end-of-school bell is a smoke detector.
It hisses and cackles, "No Escape."
Hot, September, my skin prickles with sweat.
My nose squints to separate mowed lawn from
the rancid fear I swallow.
My eyes flinch feeling the innocence of your faces.

No one has told you,
the brothers Lewis of Middletown, NJ.
You have escaped.

The TV, mostly used for fantasy GameCube battles
does its own Turn Rumble Feature **ON**/Off
Highlight SINGLE EVENT and Press **START**/PAUSE or **A** button
and makes us watch the South Tower,

where we ate pizza at S'Barro
on the 107th floor just three weeks ago, collapse.
Flame shrouded windows of disbelief
shatter our quaking hearts.
We shiver with fire,
catching each jumper mid-fall.

Ms. So-smart psychologist and super-mom
will remember the minutes
when she couldn't save anyone,
not even herself,
when she saw the powerlessness of freedom in crushing relief.

I will forget I existed before today.

Je ne comprends rien, or do I?
The bitter ozone-tinged smoke of mingled souls
coming through the screen door speaks to me:
"It is the end of school."
The bell hisses and cackles
letting them go into the September heat.

PATRICIA CARLIN

Untitled # 4

The exact morning light is two feet tall.
Oh my melancholy baby, born to be blue as the ramming sea.
Day is sealed as a sermon. It's a diversion,
not wanting to see know how light crawls away
from the garbage barge on the skittering river
rounding the tip of the island, while the streets rule and abrade.
The blue shoe of misery
holds up the walkers,
protects their skin from the rasp of pavement
so they can walk on the water of days.
Look, how the streets rebel, they say no
to the feet of the multitudes.
Through a thousand metal gratings
the underground river of noise receives the last of the day.
And there will be rejoicing in the land, a thousand tongues loosened
and filed at last to the sharp point of beginning,
just as day will shed its blowsy blue wrapper,
its bubble gum heart.

MARIE CARTIER

Me and the Big Dic Trip

My brain is LAX rush hour flight control un-patterned.
Thoughts landing: separate runways.
The last sip of coffee, heat of hidden bathroom cigarette,
Stewardess crisp, "Fasten your seat belt."
Landing finally—rough as silk.
I focus on one thought:
Muriel Rukeyser's poem, "White Space White Space Poem,"
I first read at a diner off the freeway
in Indiana, my favorite line,
"something like light stands up and is alive."

I knew I wanted her then, that white space so open,
. . . to taste the landing sweet as sandpaper
salty as Friday's working class paycheck.
I wanted Poetry—all of her virgin whore—
whose legs I would spread so wide pussy
willow that bent me sweet to submit
to the rhyme inside the big dic I caressed
plunged my hands . . .
deep into her tight edge "A" though "Z."

"Let's fuck, you sexy motherfucker," crackled
through the section headers,
the slippery syllables shook free from "S."
The big dic packed with no pretense—
she would fuck me every night.

I am Lover, midnight licks my finger
to touch low at the back forcing her pages slow.
This could go on hard. Blow. Kisses. Lover
may be in danger of falling
so deep in the dominant "T's" she will wake up
somewhere in "V," well known as little known—a dangerous 'hood.
Lover can only whisper now, mute language outside of dic,
"Voulez-vous couchez avec moi c'est soire?"

"V" winks a heavily lashed and lined eye.
Deep in the dic the silence between words
can be seductive as a shooting star:
Look at me.
Make a wish.

Lover falls through into "W," . . . 4 a.m., . . . 5 a.m.,
until in "Y" she finally . . . can trace
a kite of light . . . just bright
enough against the night . . .

I slipped through "Z." Back in flight
control. Fastened my bra and adjusted my skirt.

Announced: Runway clear. Next thought: Landing.

HELEN MARIE CASEY

Roses and Rivers

You are the river I cannot cross. Crocodiles profess your love
on both shores. They lower their eyes, smile broadly, recite poetry.
If they didn't have such bad breath, long nails, putrid skin,
and cunning in the deeps of their yes, I could almost like them.
No doubt they are delicious. I cannot get enough of you.
My eyes devour you. Skip, I call you, the name your mother
gave you even before you left her body, your cry rising
between her legs in Portland, city of roses and rivers.
You are a river where I submerge myself, crocodiles lost
in their books and rehearsals. If I were you, I would beware.
Catawampus, their scruffy legs work. We used to have wings.
We could hang from trees, at night, like lightbulbs.
Or bats. I have plagiarized you, boldly, wanting
your irrepressible song of love in every key and cranny.
You unpolish your shoes and tell me, "Helen Marie, you will never
look the part." We put on the right face, steal poems from crocodiles, fatten
the trees with babies, spackle our breaking hearts with glue, fly higher
than Colorado. *"Allons-y,"* I say, the desk applauding. *"Je ne regrette rien."*

George Chacon

You feel empty as fire—

every man who passes you by is a man who's left you behind.

Wires arc blue and electric . . .
    a season of hiccups and half-gulps
        summons the rise of acrid reflux
    clinging to the cold damp space
        under your musty lungs.

        The green flash is a rough kiss: both static and sour.

From the balcony of 381 Oak Street Elba's ghost dances and sighs,

        full as fire and music.

    Consider the snarled lines and wonky scumbled rectangles—
    a laboreal impasto of hurly-burly shapes.

The space between synapses : metronomic irregularity :

    once you thought you were really gonna walk straight into the ocean
    and come out a saint—

wash away the psycho-babble of object relations and secondary gain.

    The empty lake of love sings its blues . . .

    . . . you fill your veins with perfect saints, anointed with their perfect stains,

        grind the gleam of milky way
        and nighttime blooms of aurora borealis.

Coqui counts the crackle of cataloged defects:

    you will clap and howl until you beg midnight blue and vertigo

        wrestling with those dusty skinned ghosts.

Write letters to the editor in Sanskrit and cuneiform—
stamp them with your dental record.

"De tal palo, tal astilla,"

you are a shadow grazing on splintered walls

like the crackle left behind
by every man's footsteps.

DANIELLE COHN

Untitled

Like an angel, the woman
Passed out on the sidewalk, sporting a pair of white-feathered wings
Visions of whiskey dance in her head
Her voice like road rash, the sound of knees scraped raw
Patroness of wanderers in cities like Los Angeles
The homeless inhabit our neighborhood like stray dogs
Squatting, pants around ankles, half-hidden behind a school bus against the wall of Rite Aid
Surrounded by gobbledy-gook
They have dropped from the heavens, so they drop their pants
And the moon hits yer eye like a big piece o' sky
It's tough Amore, bitch goddess of love
Filtering down as molten lava from on high
The winged hobo-woman rises above the sidewalk surge
Hovers over Dani, the woman who stroked her curly brown hair
Paramedics will arrive soon
Beautifully harsh as a silhouette of barbed wire against the sunset
In their upside-down ambulance
No comprende she says, because none of this makes any sense
She lifts a bottle of Evian to her lips, pretends it's vodka
The homeless inhabit our neighborhood like lost gods

RITA D. COSTELLO

empty tanks by firelight

A gas-tank bass rises at the edge of the congrove, shining
like a hollow moon. Dulcimers dream of nights like this. Packed in
tents beneath the pecan trees with the smell of a Kansas fall and fire-
roasting meats. Each plucked string races the bass closer to
fusion of 70s gas-guzzling, Sherman-tank metal and the grace of
bluegrass poverty. It's a miracle of music that his fingers
aren't razor sliced and salty with blood after each song, fire-
light halos him, heals him, in protective glints off the gas
tank. He could drive to Houston on this energy, we
all could: *there's a tiger in my tank, and if there's any doubt*
when I pass you on the road you'll see his tail hanging out. I
learned how to drive here, too late in life, and outside
the bluegrass season. Well, not really learned, more like
convinced myself it was time to have a license and my own car
from behind the wheel of Carrie's battered heap, wandering
the barely-paved streets of Winfield. That was the year fire
took the lumberyard, the luminous smoke of labor, the work
of concrete hands writhing skyward in tune to the trains
and river, the darkened air fiddled and plucked fast enough to end
time. The tips of our fingers will stop the world turning, *elle*
demande un chemin âpre et épineux. Low in my chest reverberating
strings taste like love . . . just another relationship with air
and ukuleles. Swaying beside the river, even Nails softens, a girl
once driven through boards, now fluid as water. Of course
it is flat-picking that drives the water from mountain
to sea, an orchestral over-flowing of ground and hollow.

KARIN COTTERMAN

The wayward possum of life

I am alone with boxes of desire;
The breath of cardboard confuses me.
The taste of lime, trailer trucks won't stop passing by,
tires roar overhead all night long.
I smell rubber with my fingertips.

Ted stands in front of a Springfield classroom,
teaches other white people what "intercultural" means.
"You mean there's more culture than mine?"

How did I arrive here?
Down the street from Roll-N-Roll Hardee's,
the corn dog hut of my fears.
Route 66 is for traveling through, not living off of.
The cookin's warm cuz the country's cold.
The wayward possum of life.

Holiday lights make me weepy.
Let's climb the fence and live out the manger scene,
paint the figurines authentic colors.

Lilla Karin, ska du sova nu?

When I sleep there will be no dreams.
The elves carried away color and loss last night.
The boxes wrote a letter and left it on the refrigerator;
something about trucks delivering boxes of limes
that are delicious, so sweet and so cold.

CATHERINE DALY

Untitled

Love's a bird. Love's bird's
a dog-size seagull picking through garbage bins
on Santa Monica Pier,
choosing a Filet O' Fish styrofoam clamshell from the trash.

Seagull-size crows—not ravens—in the palm trees of the neighborhood
poach the mice and rats.
On legs like sophisticated black tights, they caw.

Love dies if it flies
and if it doesn't. The dull metaphorical gull
wings away to return, or yearning, close,
pulls the string on a
plot, raveling close—kiss—love's a nesting,
and nesting's eclectic. Love's collecting
feeds love's birds. Love's birds
love birds.

JENNY DAVIDSON

Plum Wine Shimmer

Her mouth is a purse
She uses burgundy lipstick only when it rains
Music shimmies through the trees
Lacy the boughs touch each other like fingertips lit
Pomegranate juice hums down my hand
I bow my head to lick the liquid
sweet like a drive to her house
She rolls in a chenille night
Moon incense wets my hair
a spiral pinecone to smell wholly
Often when I do not remember
the color of sky sings like velvet
I cannot locate Sara Vaughn in Estes Park Colorado
so I wear lipstick in the snow
bright like a cactus flower full bloom
Porcupines don't fly or they would bear fruit
Birds of a feather flock together
The nighttime blanket of sabotage makes my skin burn
Lip gloss covers the street
Her mouth turns into a diamond
She cuts her throat with her tongue
Jenny bright as a penny follows the trail where the barn was
Cut down the tree at the mouth
¿Tienes una bolsa?
Her balsa wood boat floats in a shade of wine
the suede of her hand a tight mouth pursed

JOHN DAVIS

Be There

The sky is a zebra stripe snaking down the hard flanks of night.
You are there. You have been sniffing more than roses
munching down brownies, following foghorns
in your head, seeing gentian violets.
Stop feeling velvet in your hands. It's not there.
Somewhere a trumpet blows phrases
hot as ginger taffy and you are there.
Some nights Richard Nixon is punked-out,
rising in the river mist of St. Louis
yelling *tiiiiiiiight. It's real tight*
ready to channel the Dead Kennedys and you are there
like an eagle on Sunday morning,
and Nixon's piano bench is groaning
under the weight of all the dead presidents.

Jill, in time someone will be singing
then talking fast and messy.
He will be an early myopic, drunk with fruit flies in his eyes
because he recites Homer and hits home runs
in fantasy baseball and you will be there.
You turn nineteen every day,
you can grow mold in three minutes
and still the crusty penicillin of hope
won't cure your ills. *Que puedo decir.*
I know your life is not the perfect Barbie.
Your life is the dented-boob Barbie
and Ken is waiting there in the metallic landscape
there in the trumpet phrases
there, utterly myopic with velvet hands.

JESSICA DE KONINCK

Decisions, decisions

January blows all the heat from the train
as blind men skateboard down the aisle
waving blue canes.

How long a ride to Trenton? The Conductor smiles,
Missed your exit, Jessica. After a while
smoke and mirrors carry

yesterday's vows to sleeping cars. Blame
the dead. Grandma (never) marries
grandpa. Her skin cold as cactus.

The Conductor will waltz once again.
Ah, the bittersweet lips of the ballot box.
C'est la guerre. How long a ride to Trenton.

Four turns past the exit sign.
I'm sure I've gone too far. This time
the plaid voters chant

joining the Conductor's circle dance.
In the dining car, rails smooth as gravel,
winners run a hundred miles an hour,

losers even faster. So much
commotion to stay in one place.
This week my life is canned tomatoes.

Don't pull the emergency brake.
It's only memory lost. Head north
before the weather changes.

YVONNE M. ESTRADA

My Father Sticks Up for Me at the Gates of Hell

Between Purgatory and Hell
he worked border patrol.
Relief outweighed disappointment;
crisp, khaki, flame retardant uniform
helped him feel respectable.
A line had been drawn in the sulfur;
souls in Hell were stripped hopeless,
in Limbo he waited to be prayed
into heaven.

As kids we'd recited prayers
for the dead who'd gone to Purgatory,
but I'd fall asleep, my head pressed against his chest,
rosaries droned a rumbled lullaby.
At his wake I moved worn wooden beads,
refused to chant along. Incense wafted
from a brass burner, pungent fog loud
as singed hair, melted rubber redolence
of turtle soup. "God likes this?"

A rosary unstrung, I spilled down
St. Alphonsus' front steps. Father Mathias
blessed me with a wave of his hand.
I careened toward drug rehab,
collided with the father of my future son.
Eye to a forgotten keyhole, my father watched
his daughter kick her habit post partum
in County jail, her infant become one half orphan
when the tattooed father's head gave in to a machete blow.

The key hole taunted "She needs her ass *beaten*"
in fantasy Dad grabbed her hair into one fist,
the other stuttered on her lips.
"I never hit my kids anymore."
He trained for a Main Gate position
to separate newly damned from those who
make it to Heaven on diluted Our Fathers
prayed by black veiled widows.
Fresh souls reminded him of the World:

Hollow needle slammed a brown thread
through veins, curdled blood oozed.
An old TV turned off, point of white light fades.
"I'm not waiting in this fuckin' line,"
I staggered, wasted in death.
Gruff cop-like fingers gripped my arm
propelled me to the gate to be flung inside.
A uniformed guard denied entry, argued
protocol longer than the line. Knees buckled

I rasped *"¡Ya basta, cabron!* why can't I go in?"
Angry face to face, jaw muscle bulging,
"Because you are too stupid to know where you are."
As soon as I knew him I breathed in.
His face dissolved into a paramedic's.

MARY FLORIO

The Myth of Asparagus

Asparagus is my dominatrix.
When she beats me with her stalk,
I scream,
or would if I could see straight.
She covers my eyes with a mask
that flutters and coos like a bee.
Her rubbings are mellifluous and
she tastes extremely raw, like
someone my beloved Hamlet might
take to task in one of his
breezier Danish soliloquies.

I think I am falling out of love with Hamlet.

And what is love anyway, but
a googol of one-liners? Everyone
loves a lothario—who knows
women better? Not for nothing,
but oh how I long to walk
the wet dog of desire, how
I long to wear the scabs of love!

I think Hamlet would enjoy
a spanking from a Tudor queen—
she'd melt him back to manhood,
or something like it. I'd like
to think the stars aren't crossed
for anyone, and me in particular,
that vegetable love might grow
vaster than empires, like the
holy asparagus, which comes
back for more no matter how
many times you take your
pleasure. Et cetera.

"I would die for my art," she says.

The Greeks called her bed a crown
and built her many walled gardens,
and she will bloom for 15 years
or more, they say,
sprouting ferns and berries
between the hard, quick rise
of her breeding seasons.

Cherryl Floyd-Miller

bountiful

how we heap and dip and cup
under covers, a herd of sleeping spoons,
bellies ballooned with the good times.

this isn't a year we merely crave the ghost
of yam syrup at our noses
or gawk at thirty-second ads of basted thighs
and honeyed breasts on a fat clucker.

this year, we poke the gluten between
elastic cells of yeast rolls,
ears arcing for narrative that descends
like pine cones from the needles.
we burn a few taste buds
waiting for a blade to slice our bird,

whiffs of every morsel in our memories
dripping from our famished fingers.

remember Bubba Pugh selling pickled
pigs feet and penny candy in Lincoln Heights?

we were hungry
and so full we brewed a phlegm
in the throat and diaphragm.

we freaked our familiar—
the electric slide, the Bankhead bounce,
rhythm just the ricochet of chow in the backbone

no lookie-lookie, no getie-getie[1]

the canary bow of grace in us
makes us each a Saturn and a sun,
grinning stars sink their rodent teeth into us.

we stretch our corn husk scalps
over turkey bones and beat the moon.
Sweet Pea winces at the first blow
she will swallow the chime and thud
of next November:
rerun turkey anything and mutual cranberry stew.

we are determined to recycle
what is missing in us
embrasse-moi jusqu'au nous furieux[2]

what a gravy can whisper
into the hollow of a rib—

what design to raise the spoons.

[1] *West Indian saying that means "If you don't look for trouble, you won't find it." My African American equivalent: "Don't start none, won't be none," sometimes chanted during friendly, competitive dancing among my relatives and friends.*

[2] *This French phrase translates "embracing the me in the furious us."*

KATE GALE

Jagged Pieces of Language

See that kite, honey? Life's like that.
You stringing along, nobody really watching.
The air very cold. Talk to God, plum cake.
It planned this.
It on its cold, rosy throne.
Throwing out jagged pieces of language.

Let there be this.
Let there be that.
Raising its dark hands.
Batter my heart, three-personed God, somebody asked.
Well, the average human gets that wish.
Gets battered.

The clouds hanging overhead,
laugh at you, stringing along.
Like an explosion.
A lightning storm would amuse.
You will be cold.
You will be hot.

The air will taste salty or wet.
Or grimy as the case may be.
You will see blue.
The earth will move violently.
You will feel air and water rushing.
The way to control your flight is not to control it.

Only Calvinists believe that.
We aren't kites on a string.
Far from it.
Kites have their own little souls,
held in the cup of someone's hand
while the kite is bucked about.

We are dreamers so dreams dream us.
Nothing happens we didn't design.
Give God a tall order.
Ask for a baby, a lover, a million bucks.
Mon Dieu est si grand, si fort et si puissant.
It won't hear a thing you say

It's doing its funky hair in its funky sky
while you're praying. It's doing fujimama.
You will pray at some time in your life.
Then you'll make something happen.
Or you won't.
If you do, you'll tell yourself God did it.

It will do the fujimama some more, so go figure.
It's about as interested in your little life as smog is.
You want to change your life?
Prayer wouldn't be the first best step.
You'll find creative dreaming goes further
than blue nights praying.

Downwind of you someone is helplessly leaning into the stars
whispering, I am a kite and it isn't my fault.
Katydid dreamed that once.
Nothing good ever happened by dreaming
except for Martin Luther King in Alabama
or Ghandi.

Nothing else.
Much.
Ever.
You will carry your soul around in a small twisted
paper bag asking God every day how to change it
into a swan, a dirty bird, but you don't know that.

God will have Its hair done up in dreadlocks.
The world was without form and void.
Darkness was upon the face of the deep.
God said, Let there be light.
Light feels like a whack in the head some mornings,
especially if you're hung over.

The crowded places in our minds where dreams hang out.
Transformation dreams get eaten by.
Soup crackers cops sirens radio freeways appointments.
Transformation dreams get eaten by.
Yellow-bellied bomb freaks people with expensive hair
guys asking for gas money to spend on a smoke.

I am not a box kite myself. I'm a rainbow dragon kite
with a long tail. When the wind stops, I fly along
on my own power pausing now and then to change direction
or to pray for wind or light. If the wind doesn't come,
I say, Let there be wind. Or light. Whichever I want first.
Kites flying loosely screaming out the name of God.

RICHARD GARCIA

Crepuscule in Blue or Green

The evening is a poem extending itself across and down
the page of the sky. The sun slips tenuously into the ocean
like a squirrel stealing peanuts from the pocket of a man asleep
under a tree in a park by an airport. You can count on squirrels
to know the difference between a wallet and a bag of peanuts.
The tiny hairs inside my ears vibrate when I see you
sitting in front of the computer painting your toenails blue
or green. I get confused between blue and green
in the evening when I taste the approach of night
sliding down my skin through the forest of my arms.
Mr. Squirrel lives in a hole in a tree in Clover Park.
I should not be mistaken for this squirrel that crawls
into pockets nor am I the man under the tree who is only
pretending to be asleep although he is dreaming.
If you read this line out loud backwards you will say,
"say will you backwards loud out line this read you if,"
which could cause a disruption in the syntax of the universe,
not to mention consciousness and you'd inhale aluminum
through your eyes and be mistaken for a language poet.
Notice the way music, for instance, Monk's Crepuscule With Nellie,
proceeds across the evening in stately shades of gray,
with some blue or green causing you to remember someone
you've never met, standing at a window in an apartment house
you've never seen in a place you've never been and you'll feel
a nostalgia of memory and desire. But if you're strolling in the park
you might hear the gardener, the one from Papua, New Guinea,
say with disgust, as he stoops behind a hedge, "Yuck, *gumi bilong kok.*"
and not have the slightest idea what he was talking about.
O the rubbery hammer of language, the shoes of doom and the painful
St. Sebastian pincushion knowledge that you know nothing,
nothing—the piercing vision when you smell a memory.
And the heart, the heart is not the organ of love, all it knows
is bumpa-bumpa-bump, bumpa-bumpa-bump. Give me the liver
for love and I will love you with all my liver for all my life
for I can turn myself inside out. I can be so small I can nap
curled up between your little toe, the one with the nail too small
to paint, and the one next to it that Ricky Ricardo, also known
as El Machete, likes to roll his tongue around while pretending your toes

are his harmonica. Someday, in the distant future, a holographic
image of your toes painted blue or green will be on display
in an ethnographic museum where they will be labeled incorrectly
as primitive musical instruments played by oiled squirrel worshippers
in a park near an airport. For the truth of time is in the porridge,
or as the bible says, *Bereshit bara Elohim et hashamayin ve'et ha'arets,*
suggesting that gods and goddesses created heaven and earth together.
And the squirrel, as the sun setteth, sitteth on the cyclone fence
with his paws in prayer and sayeth amen. That's when all the cats
on the block come out to the front lawns and sit still for quite
a long while facing what remains of the sun like Egyptian statues.

RYN GARGULINSKI

Bing Cherries are Stravinsky

Bing cherries are Stravinsky
they taste like his toes
their ripeness makes loud jarring sounds—
cold—discordant—atonal as a humid day they
don't taste like his toes—they taste like
his fingers—lithe, lean, bold little hands
making a piano hum, a warm toast blanket of mussed
hullabaloo—because Mom never let us play with guns—
raise the rent on the voices in your head
The bleak bathwater of ideology!
A piercing cat's purr invades us,
persuading our actions—my brother took his head off,
left it for The Doors—Kamikaze took the mike,
her eyes ran wildly as she looked to the left—
she will move to New York—where she lives fitful
and mean in a large shoebox, an apartment she got
from the classifieds, a person alive but
listed in obituaries—*Oui, concierge, j'habite ici*—
where stairs glower and moan where floorboards whistle in pain
under the strain, stain and splatters of Stravinsky.

PAMELA GARVEY

The Raining of Her Hair

The raining of her hair onto his chest,
when they made love, singed his skin;
scarred it with lines lighter than rain
and softer than her honey scent.
It's the smell that scarred him,
staying long beyond her
and untouchable, like the whisper
of her hair tumbling.
It still wakes him each night,
his own salt sweat on his tongue.
Sleepless without her, he listens
to Johnny Cash singing to prisoners
in San Quentin, the whole place
whooping it up, thrilled and pissed.
Poor Johnny, now palsied and guitarless,
sickens because of loss,
the way it thunders
even in the neighbor crooning to her wailing infant:
Baby Daddy ain't comin' home no more.
He hates that song as much as the blue flame of love
making ash out of hearts;
its heat deadly as spring, the season
when he blooms anew from the mulberry,
gets to stain somebody's sidewalk.
He's become the berries that can't be eaten.
Without regret he spits at the sunlight
greening the rest of the world.
And he's sick of writers like this one,
Poet-Lips, narrating over his shoulder.
Come spring, just to spite them, he'll saw away
the mulberry's branches, stack them for winter
because he doesn't need poetry
and its stressed buds to exist
en medio de un amor doloroso. *
Really, what he needs is a dog,
some Rin Tin Tin to save the day,
lick his hands clean
with the healing tongue that pants

forget her, forget her, forget her.
Rhythmic as the rain when it storms.

* From Pablo Neruda's "The Poet"

Suicide Easter Egg

The fog this morning was like soupy pee,
though the fire engines stayed red right through it.
Women ogled me as I slipped on ice
that crackled like castanets, their perfume
hot as butter on biscuits.
Rayford Wright was the Biscuit Eating Champion
of Hattiesburg, Mississippi, where all the houses
are painted yellow, the way
what pens don't write in daylight
glows at night like embers, like
the corn a blind chicken pecks.
But the gray horses of wisdom are asleep
in the stables of impropriety,
and snakes sing Puccini in the dry grass
by the road, while old Junior is croaked
to the eyes in a lily pond.
One day his gigabytes will rust green.
Ou sont les neiges d'antan, he croons
as the trees roll their own joints,
the corn has a finger in every ear,
and the rising sun blushes like a fire engine.

John Grey

Swamp Life

The swamp is the belching belly of the world.
I have a 'gator for a gut.
I can taste the swirl of brown,
Scour the ceaseless appetite of wading birds,
Hear the drowning cry of tree-root
Sweat the air's thickness on my skin,
Smell the death perfume of slow meandering rivers.
'Gators sound like heat looks,
like Jenny Black back in Boston
who got thick mangroves close to me;
no, not this close, never this close.
Beer sure tastes good at Harry's shack,
sitting on the wooden porch,
shooting the breeze, cracking on the locals,
getting drunk from being northerners.
"If July was a direction,
it'd point you to South,"
somebody said to me once.
The seething rocks of anger and stupidity
poke through the liquid skin.
Life is as fluid as sidewalks.
I adorn myself in shanties and stock-cars.
Lord John is as delirious as a corpse in mud.
A year from now, there'll be 'gators
teaching middle school, 'gators serving behind the bar
well-heeled 'gators spending swamp dollars,
rouge-red 'gators of the night hustling tricks.
'Gators will be more human than the tourist boats.
Bonne chance, mes cretins.
Lizards solve crosswords in the dusk,
owls square dance with mice,
dragon-flies write poems on frog-skin.
And the swamp belches 'gator mating cries.

DINA HARDY

Stitching Up the Past

El mundo es un pañuelo, "It's a small world." Spanish, Lit:
'The world is a handkerchief.' Grooved pie, v. pt., slang, to leave

The past is a handkerchief he irons, folds four times,
then tucks into his breast pocket. The sludge of
hours-old coffee varnishes his tongue as he takes a swig.
Constant humming comes from the fish tank. By the door,
a cat sleeps, nose open to the threshold, the smell of wet earth.
Outside, rain dances across pavement like oil on a searing skillet.

He pats down the lump of fabric over his heart, feels
picket fences and lemonade on a day hotter than this one,
perched on a porch swing, on Spencer Avenue
in Batchelor, Louisiana, about to pop the question
to Sharon Barron. That was a beautiful day. That was
the worst day of his life, but in captivity, goldfish stop growing
when they reach four inches. They expand three-fold
if they can escape domestication. Really, it was a relief
she said *No.* So, he grooved pie out of the south and settled west
because that's where the sun sleeps and he needed the light.
Mira, chico, there was nothing left to do but buy a bible.

Blind eyes of time, thick with cataracts and the sharp focus
that comes with news that your first love has died. He feeds
the fish with memories, turns the cat to air, leaves,
then crosses paths with Diana, his neighbor,
who was Sharon's best friend in college,
because after all, it *is* a small world. She was the one
who broke the news to him this morning, now declares,
Any doubts you may have will disappear
early next month, as if this cardboard wisdom
will transform the pain into linen.

El mundo es un pañuelo, he thinks. His car embraces him
while the rain plays jazz, beats syncopation on the windshield.
The corners of his world have been unraveling for awhile,
until now, he convinces himself, now as he weaves
into rush hour traffic to retrace the creases of the last forty years.

PATRICIA HARRELSON

Apron Strings

The household wrapped around her, tied with bow—then knot.
Mother was splattered with cloying displeasure:
ammonia fumes steaming from the diaper pail
broken glass clattering across linoleum
bobbin tension pulling tight stitches
blood dripping from wounded finger
her frustration sucked on until foil
crumpled electrically under her tongue
when Janis Joplin drove a psychedelic Porsche through San Francisco.
The stitches weren't tight enough; the machine in want of servicing,
but the lolo dude stayed tweaking at his stereo
so she peeled onions to cry for her babies—
to tune in "yo mama's so fat she always look like she pregnant."
The sooty refrain of blame clicked like marbles in her skull
in a game that forbade any losers
while the dishwasher churned forth the best meal of the week.
You can see that Patsy had spun her apron into a cocoon.
I think she will eat through cotton thread expecting silk.
The svelte table will announce her outing:
"Give the woman room to succor angst."
Que será será
whisper the down-fluffed quilts slipping rest from the knot.

Stephanie Hemphill

Prayer

A twist of smoke, I rise
from extinguished match,

live in a place you cannot touch,
inch between thighs.

Carbon on nightstand, sulfur on lips,
soundless splash of lost quarter

tossed into wishing well,
my voice repeats then diminishes.

Because Alice shrank in Wonderland,
I drink cherry juice,

slide down hole and cannot rise.
Yet on the third day he rose again

so that guilty fingers smell
like incense, taste like cunt.

The man in the glass room
always says "Yes," then slips

into high heels, the three-pronged
bishop of better not tell.

I carry an ocean of sand in my pocket,
ask not to be called beauty.

He tells me my hands are small
as baby spoons, and Sunday

will forgive my fingerprints and dirty skirts.
His silent hands loosen the rosary

around my neck. Black beads unwhisper
notre padre as they fall off chain,

roll between slats of metal grate.
I fall to knees, search

in darkness for the pill
that will make me large.

MICHAEL HOERMAN

Pentecost

When the moon glows
Like a firebug's belly, I poke it
And write poems on your eyelids
With the juice, my fingers
Grubby, like a little boy's.

That's how you get your poems.

For payment, I whisper
Into your ear. You never stir,
But I leave richer than a Rockefeller,
And sleep until 10 a.m.
"Bankers' hours," the laureled poets say,
Huddled, down at the Grolier,
Counting their change
After the trains stop running.

I strut by, like a cock
With a golden song.
The ching-ching of my razor spurs
Means money in the bank
And a song on your page.

NOAH HOFFENBERG

Inner Chatter

Everyone knew the experiment went horribly wrong
when the man's clone began to grow inside himself.
Like the brother who lived inside his brother's swollen head
doling out the intermittent migraine.
Under his skin, he felt the squirming of worms
or something wormlike anyway.
At least that's what it looked like,
while he watched the undulations
just beneath his dermis.
The man could smell someone other than himself
very close by, no more than a breath's breadth away.
When he would touch his own skin,
the thing underneath felt like grasping at gefilta fish
in a jar of aspic. And tasted like it too.
Was the voice he heard his own voice,
or was it a voice that seemed independent
of the man's thought processes?
The man occasionally felt the screams of his inner twin
vibrating off his sternum. Or was it gas?
It wasn't so much a twin or a clone, really,
in as much as the man's twin was a tumor.
In the voice of Big Arnold: *It's not a tumor!*
There are innocent people down there. Chill out.
The body creates tumors so they must be good for you.
I do not know from what you are saying?
The slippery viscera of truth
fed the man's symbiant buddy.
The tumor's teeth were porous, yet fully developed.
There was no sign of plaque because the teeth
were attached to the jaw in the man's gut.
In the past the jaw had clacked with the mandible,
but the man chalked it up as a crackily back.
The Jew had no real prospects to speak of,
but he would survive nonetheless.
At least he would have his health.
The man would have to use his talis
as a conservative tourniquet to tie around the seppuku.
Tumors are just late developing organs, the man said.

Baruch attah adonai, elohaynu meloch ha'Olam,
boray p'rei hagafen.
The pickling jar filled with formaldehyde said, *ahhh*.
The man's teeth chattered, but he could not be sure
that they were his own choppers.

ABHA IYENGAR

Dove-tailed to You No More

Peaceful as a dove I sit
Immovable,
Without wings.
I look outside the window
Snowflakes fall cool against my skin.
They taste like melted butter
As I lick them away
The smell of pines assails my nostrils
And I hold a flake in my hand
To draw it all in,
Even as I listen quietly
To the soft falling snow
My fingers reach out blindly
To connect with its whispering sighs.

Oh, Vinod! Wildflower Hall at Simla
Stolen moments
Of strawberries and cream
Don't take away the dreams of yesterday
To bring home the reality of today.

"'Zzup?" you ask.
Well, I wonder if tonight
You will launch yourself into space
To pluck me periwinkles from the sky
Which are blue because your eyes are blue.

We sometimes have to be cruel to be kind
I know what you have in mind
Sharp knived words to cut through already bleeding flesh
Wounded by unspoken thoughts.
Your softness is like a diamond
Your caress an attempt to trample
All over Tuntunia.

I envision myself as the dove
Who drops the heavy leaf of peace
From its beak
In order to fly away
I know not where.
Kya pata kahan?
Perhaps where the leaves of happiness will embrace me
And the wings of love will attach themselves to me
Help me soar in the arms of the wildness beyond—
A wildness beyond
My dreams
Of strawberries and cream.
It could be
Of snowflakes and red cherries.
Whatever.

Oh yes! The dove does have wings
Watch it fly away
Chasing the periwinkles in an azure sky.
I close the window and leave
The soft snow falls silently around me.

ROBIN JACOBSON

The Opposite of Seeds

I sort through my life like so many apples,
toss aside suffering as though it were rotten or green,
as though a worm could be wrong in the eating
or the sweet bite save me from my own core.
We're the only tree that eats its own fruit,
says the Sherpa when we stop to rest.
If we walk too fast, we'll leave our souls behind.
Fortunately, the lost train of thought
pulls into the station in the middle of the night
and even this far north the sun comes again,
baring the bodies of infants pressed under the snow
to die. The opposite of seeds.
Fortunately, I am not one of those buried,
not Anastasia—though they call me Princess.
This year the princess has turned into an onion,
hardier, something that can take the cold
and the heat. Dante would be proud.
I can almost hear him scribbling:
In the middle of the journey of my life
I found myself in darkening woods,
my way on the path lost. Oh, those woods—
savage and rough and loud—even now,
remembering, my eyes widen with fear. . . .
Actually, it's a relief to blink first, finally stop
squinting against the sun as it stares
through a hole in the ozone like an eye
without lids. Eyes closed,
I feel my ears grow long as rhododendron leaves,
twitch visibly with the slightest rustle.
I let the world have its way—
patio sheened with moss and grass, weeds greening
everywhere a tremor has opened the earth
a blade's width. If I leave it a season or two,
it will regress to wild, like a small child
left to his own devices. Sam curls up in my lap,
still sleepy and pajama-warm, asks me before I go,
Where's the Wailing Wall? I can see it
in the desert—tears, oceans, how whales would

write the history of the world if only they had thumbs.
Echo in my chest, the god Doctor had me swallow
radioactive chocolate to see if he could see the hole
in my heart. I was only five, hooked words like strange
fish as they swam by—*congenital, functional,*
healed over like ice on a fishing hole. Still
I live with echoes. Florence: at the *pensione* I dream
Leonardo's dreams, flying machines
trying to lift off from the parchment like fantastic
insects. They bump along my arms and I slap them down
with gusts and gravity. Their mangled wings.
I wake to the smell of burnt ink
and earth. Somewhere beyond the garden,
Adam and Eve are still making love, forgetting
the new technology. Eve's pacemaker
pops from its housing, swings inside her
like an apple on a branch end in a breeze.
The beat goes on. They don't stop till they've come.
She calls the god Doctor, who finally gives her
a choice. She leaves things dangling.

Rhoda Janzen

Deceitful Beyond All Cure

Snug as a swim-cap, the cat on your head avers,
Idling would stall any engine but mine.
Risk is to fear what worship is to shrine,
replies the beaded naval ornament. The cat purrs,
etcetera, in the direction of the beads. *Form*
follows function! say the beads (green, idyllic.)
The blanket interrupts the cat with warm acrylic:
Detachment, of course, protects the charm
of anagnorisis. The paw on your lobe's pure
as a square or a post-it note: funeral at eight,
wake at six, dead at forty-four. *Where's the wait:*
the heart, you say, *is deceitful beyond all cure.*
A trench coat parts the blinds like legs—goddamn,
it's only daylight getting hard for one more ma'am.

ALLISON JOSEPH

Collision

You're the slinky shoe I yearn to wear,
a violin so rare it's not been made.
You're bee sting and precious honey,
purple bruise and radio static.
You're a broken vial of pheremones
spilled on my velvet kitchen floor.
For you, I'm Pavlov's dog, barking
and twitching in a Moscow kennel.
You're salt and vinegar, chips
I can't stop munching even though
I know carrots are better for my figure,
my eyes. You bring the noise, the funk,
the juice, make me quiver with a shiver
of your tongue. If you're a god,
then I can't sin. One monkey don't
stop no show, but the hard elbow
of lust can sure stop me, wake me
from slumber like a melody crooned
by witches. For you, I'm naked
in Trafalgar Square, little Miss
Goody Two Shoes bare for her man.
And joy will thrive in sinew and eardrum.
You sexy confection, you make me
re-live heaven. Take me slowly,
then *allegro, allegro*, make the roots
of dahlias quake. Shattered, you're all
over me, and I don't mind the fracture.

GINA LARKIN

Lilacs in the Outfield

Lotion slides across my skin like a lover's hands,
repeats my name in seven languages,
filling the space around me
with lilacs and chocolate.

That spot behind my knees throbs
as the sheen moves up my thigh.
I suck air like a lollipop
tasting the lilac's bark.

It's spring—Brooklyn—
a stoop across from Ebbets Field,
and Sonny Fisher is kissing my neck.

It is not spring—
no lilacs at all,
and every ball designed to discombobulate
to turn my head into a bat.

That's amore! the umpire shouts.
The crazy glue of love sticks the split
skull back together,
makes heartbreak the goal.

With his every touch,
lilacs bloom from the concrete.
I feel the power
that will turn other Sonnys
into warty princes.

Kisses are love, *mon amie,*
as any frog will tell you—
just beware the rock hard
candy of a first lover's touch.

MICHAEL LASSELL

The Day George Harrison Died

Grey is the daughter of grieving and whey,
which is why it is spelled (contrary to Webster) in the English manner—
with a vowel as empathic as mercy or ease:

Exxon, elephant, elegant/e-mail, entering, earnestly, eggs.

Grey smells like the smoke off the low-tide Thames,
tastes like riverbanks curdling in an acrid urban breeze,
(the fetid sound of a brackish backwater).

The mudlarks will be picking tears out of the mire with their cod heads and penny pieces.

Remember the time by Lake Moraine when a boy whose name
is frequently forgotten—was it David, and something Anglo-Saxon?—
smoked dope and curled in my arms for hours, his granny glasses
clouded over with our shared heat (the misted eyes of a wiser owl who
bids adieu to common knowledge)?—

unless it was a Mersey's idle dream:

dahlia, difficult, dominoes/dik-dik, diptych, dipstick, dregs.

Some nights there's nothing on cable,
not even the BBC, for which you are paying *mucho dinero.*
For you, the red, white and blue will always be British:
Bobby blue, hoarfrost white on the morning fields of
Stratford one Thanksgiving Thursday in your youth,
and red phone boxes—or Twizzlers as you wait for a movie
you don't want to see while soggy strangers munch popcorn:

pumping, petticoat, platypus/primavera, panoply, pegs.

It's because you haven't got a thing to wear
that your peppers failed to germinate;
you can taste your tongue and it's zincky, sour.

"Don't make me take you to church, young man!"
the turbaned Caribbean TV psychic warns.
Her voice is fruity, flutelike, bloated on the fumes of something fishy.

The embrace of leather and absence is that
of a father whose love is late and suspect:
it's as warm as November and as awkward.

I went up to him, once, just pulled his arm and said
"I love you," and he smiled at me, so I kissed his glamorous brocade:

broken, baklava, Benjamin/bluebottle, blushing, Boston, begs.

(Wee Mickey was the only one who got to call him Geordie.)

Oh, yes, there will be bad hair days to come. Fat days.
Endless afternoons when you haven't got a book to read or
a friend who isn't out of town on some fabulous vacation.
It will be August all year long, insufferable, *ad infinitum.*

Once again the brutal dove of peace has come to rest
on your frail broad shoulder, and you want to pull the weeping sheets
up to your grizzled chin, hitting the snooze button over and over again
until a sodden supper of takeout sesame chicken

chuckling, canopy, kaffeeklatsch/Caspian, canticle, kaffiyeh, kegs.

Not knowing him was the way he loved me.

"Verloren ist das Schlüsselein,"
the unsurprisingly dour day drawls in all
the colors of London's lost Victorian fog.
"Forgotten is the little key," you think to your earlier self,
chilled to the wishbone in the after-opera Berlin snow.

"How can you possibly be bored with all
those toys in your room?" is the echo
choking back from my childhood like
an oily bog that double-troubles up
the clogging pipes of my unscoured sink.

But that's *not* how you felt, or feel even now, unless
they mean some other kind of bored, like drilled or *chewed,*
as if you are a bower of trees in the Indonesian
summer, now riddled with the snaking borrows
carved by ravenous maggots (the way you exhausted
would-be lovers with a hunger of your own), and the burly trees are
about to fall, prey to steaming slow disintegration,
fading from proud ebony—erect above the canopy—to ovoid oblivion
crashing in a cloud of ash or slate or charcoal grey no one will hear.

Yet saffron, rarest spice of all, is found in the common crocus flower,
ground from its viscous gold stigmata, where pollen falls to germinate
like dust motes in a shaft of sun on sated lovers' tangled legs.

BETTY LIES

Viva

The past is a book of empty pages—
nobody ever really lived in it. Try to imagine
Verdi and his Giuseppina
at their mustard-yellow villa in Busseto,
lying dark, sated with sex,
sniffing the strange perfume
coming off each other's music,
townspeople scribbling *Viva Verdi*
on the walls, or Shakespeare
about to brush the dust of Stratford off his jerkin,
screwing Anne in the next-best bed
as toads and bugs *thunk* from the thatch,
downstairs the old folks nodding
around the ingle. Picture your parents
licking chocolate off each other, or
heaven forbid, your mother's fragrant sigh
as Little B starts waiting
in the wings. She'll make an entrance
on the stage of instantly-the-past,
play a short love scene, say some lines,
forget the rest, go off.
When did the moon get full again,
spilling its cup of borrowed light
as if that petty glare could clarify,
illuminate, convince you anything
was ever real? None of it happened,
all of it is happening, it's done with mirrors,
strings of them, wavy and fogged,
reflecting everything at once,
the nothing that is there.
And even as you're writing new scripts
with the sharp pencil of *now*
a big white gum eraser follows close behind
and the moon struts its pocky show
against the seamy backdrop of the dark.

DIANE LOCKWARD

Felis Rufus

When his teacher forces similes,
  my small son writes, *I am wild
    as a bobcat.* He has the sleek

      body, muscular limbs of a cat,
    the salty kiss. Curled in a corner,
  he pretends he's a kitten born

blind. Nights, he sleeps like a boy,
    thumb in his mouth, limbs twitching.
      Days, he romps in woods, chases

      chipmunks and birds, comes home
    dusted with duff. He grows greedy
for meat, feeds on chickens, rabbits,

and squirrels, collects feathers
    and bones. His rust-colored hair thickens,
      each day more beautiful, more terrifying.

      Long-legged, feet padded, he ravages
    furniture, prowls the neighborhood
from dawn until dusk. Once he brings

home a lamb, once a young pig. My child
    disappears into the rocky hillside, paces
      the jagged ledge of his difference. Do I

      only imagine tufted ears, cheek
    ruffs? My lynx-eyed son, my wild
boy. Nothing can hold him.

Sometimes he comes back
    as a boy, still calling me Muvver.
      Sometimes the house fills with the must

      of his fur. Sometimes night breaks
    with mournful howls, cantillations
come down from cold, dark hills.

JOEL T. LONG

The Sleep of Painted Angels

Her eyelids are blankets still wet from rain.
Her eyes sleep within them like old flutes or tin.
The air tastes of artichoke that we peel down
like the leaves of a book until we get to the heart
that burns like burnished green incense, soft as ash,
quiet as feathers in a porcelain bowl. Taddeo Gaddi
might have painted her sleeping in Florence,
but the air then would have been loud with the noise
of Savanorola damning beauty with a fork and fire.
Savanarola was buff when it came to religious fanaticism
and fear, and all the Florentines wore red in his behalf.
When they burned him, the doves left town for three years,
and brought back in their talons a sow's ear sewn with gold embroidery
into the closed eye of benevolence. So she sleeps
the sleep of rats, nestled in wood shavings so low
they seem a warm bit of hollow air. She rises into
somnambulism to sit at the old desk and write out
whole passages of the Book of Job in the original Hebrew.
And when she finishes a page, she puts down the pen
and kisses her fingers as though she were drawing her lips
along the edge of a blade. When she rises again, she speaks.
Joey will break into a thousand pieces which will grow wings
like moths and scatter into the four lights with dread pleasure
of disintegration. She is made of vaporous stone and bee sound.
Ella quiere a dormir. The mirrors lead her back into our bed,
and she is repainted there in olive light. She could stay for years.

JANET McCANN

The Heavy Gloves of Conscience

Her mouth is a tunnel on the Pennsylvania Turnpike
and she has swallowed my flashlight.
How tepid those lines smell, their acrid textures leaking motor noise
　　　and light—
an oily reek of yellow,
not at all like "Kurt Vonnegut is a carton of brown yoghurt."
No, not tepid precisely, but sallow.
I love this town,
though it has a high incidence of alopecia
because of the rabid skunks that roam the main streets.
Look, low-tech stuff is what I'm really about.
The heavy gloves of conscience . . .
Her heart of gold rattled and clanked in her chest
as she gobbled the world atlas and all the guidebooks.
Lacey, how are you ever going to unpack this,
nothing will ever be the same again.
Oh, the plaid predictions of grandmothers!
The instruction manual was full of uncertainties.
O dieses is das Tier, das es nicht gibt . . .
The phone book screams, torn in two by feelings.
At the end of the tunnel, an asshole. Light filtered through that.

FRANCES RUHLEN McCONNEL

We Dream of Heroes

Deep in a bramble-bush of stars,
we crouch, quivering. A screech owl
wickers above us, her talons
lift what might be our fluttering hearts aloft
to the hollow in the great white spire
of the dead pine where her chicks
open their black throats
to murky sleep. In our mouths,
a taste of dying campfires. On our backs
the harsh rasp of sunburn.

We dream of that hero, our father,
that Maker of Bombs, Hank Ruhlen,
who jacked up the corner of the shed
that was listing toward Lake Watts Bar
and dropped it on his foot.
We're dreaming of his three toes,
black as talons, the bones shattered
like coke bottles under truck wheels;
how all he said was "Gol-darn it!"

Fish doze in the armbones of the pine
since they raised the water at Watts Bar.
Mud sleeps in the cabin, mud oozing slow
as smoke from shit, as Mom said
her Pa used to say, who maybe
learned it from his Pa,
who gave his grandkids coffee,
including the baby (our mother),
hardly before she was weaned,
coffee mud-thick with sugar and fresh cream.
Coffee, he claimed, kept him alive
in the Union prison, when food ran out.

But maybe the shit off which
smoke steamed so slow in the saying
was the hot shit of fear
dropped in the dewy dawn
before the Battle of Shiloh,
where soldiers like exiled kings
fell to kiss the fetid ground and all day
guns racketed from the banks
of the old wild Tennessee,
far under these blood-warm lakes.

Oh, memories of memories like the winking of fireflies,
what is your cipher? What myths shape your constellations?
Oh, whip-poor-will—*Caprimulgus vociferous*—
we wish on your first call at dusk
("Cuck-rhip-oor-ree")
to be like that hero, our father, who fought in no war
except the one against his sons and daughter,
but stoic as a man in a lab-coat,
gave up his life to Uranium 235
and the plant run by Watts Bar Dam kilowatts.

We dream of his bones and our mother's,
deep in a bramblebush of stars,
glowing like boughs in dark water.

Julia McGarey

Guilt Trip

Her mind was as hazy as her contacts.
Her hand brushed the wallpaper,
She could almost taste it.
She sent sparks through her eyes,
Burned down the house.
The grass shot cold through her bare feet.
The sirens sang her to follow the ambulance.
She paused at the sight of the inverted car,
Licked the hot, salty red from her fingertips,
Stole the blood-sweat smell from the scene.
She knew it was her fault as soon as she saw him on the stretcher.
But it wasn't her fault.
She stepped from the yard to the hospital room in one movement.
Sliding home, summer baseball days.
"No thanks Delmar, a third of a gopher would only
Arouse my appetite without beddin' her back down."
Leslie couldn't stand Mississippi anymore.
She had developed a sense of the word cowabunga,
Had nightmares of betrayal in red white and blue.
All she could do was tell Jules.
A year from now you'll know.
The truth will be clearer than the dirt under your fingernails.
The rioting dogs will grin from behind bars:
        Cave canem.
The willowy branches of disdain
Will call you through the mouth of the refrigerator,
Shelves lined in fingernail dirt,
Red, white and blue.

PHIL MEYER

Ravishing

I slip
the poet
part of me
an occasional back
room glory hole blow job. But
he's born
again, wants
to be man and
wife. Still, I shilly shally
about, a lolligagger gagging
on his artsy
tang

that tastes like Ella singing Blow Ill Wind at Carnegie Hall in nineteen eighty-eight before she lost her leg but after her sight had failed. WAIT! It was A Tisket, A Tasket. I saw that brown and yellow basket in a whole new light.

What if
he grabs for
good, guts me
with his gusty pen?
Sluiced by a
gush of
words
I'd sit nervy
and jangling, white
knuckles against
a belly full to
birthing.

Mister Pea Pod shucked to life.

NO!
      I will
            fight
                  the veiny,
                         uncut cock
                                 of inspiration,
                                          a spinster
                                                soldier.

                                 The battle to be won is
                                 one that can't be wan.
                                 Es un problema grande
                                 este separacion della
                                 persona.

  As the paper before me u
                        n
                      z
                    i
                 p
                  s
                  mumbles a black-blind melody,
                  his velvet scent befuddling . . .

"Oh why was I so careless with that basket of mine?"

PEGGY MILLER

Education

October third, wind in the grass,
like Grandma's hairbrush ripping out the knots.
Grandma said Lu-Maid wine cheese is the best
foot cream you can buy. Even at the thought,
my toenails could taste it, taste Grandma's
sharp voice warning little fingers away
from her knick-knacks.

It wasn't October at all.
It was forever. It was now, Grandma
hemming our skirts in the morning,
fast, so we wouldn't miss the bus.
Never pants: girls couldn't wear pants to school.

Once I did that—
forgot to change out of my play pants
and wore them to school, afternoon session
because it was so crowded.
And I trembled and cried and refused
to take off my coat. I went to the Nurse's office.
She gave me a big green corduroy skirt,
a diaper pin at the waist, out of the charity box.
Billy Mundhausen called them dung-clothes.
Grandma said if you wear dung-clothes
tomatoes will never ripen in your garden
and I believed her.

I believed everything,
my mind a big purple sink of hunger.
She said you have to eat a peck
of dirt before you die. She said
if you hit your mother your arm
will stick out of the grave. She said
a dirty washrag behind the outhouse
will get rid of your warts. She said
if you build a barn on Sunday it will not stand,
and if you sew on Sunday
you will have to take the stitches out
with your nose in hell.

The front porch was closed in. Evenings
there Grandma sat stitching the gold tassel edge
back onto the Salvation Army flag
while I sculpted headless Greek
nudes out of gray kindergarten clay.

JEFF MOCK

Masculinity in Springtime

Spring struts in like John Wayne in a tutu.
The saloon doors swing open on danger
And delight. Everybody looks good
In a tutu, even Woodrow, my dog. Try it.
Put one on. The elastic clings to your waist.
The tulle rustles soft as rain and flavors
The shocked air. Its taste is a sweet pleasure.
Check the mirror above the bar, boy,
And turn a turn. Dance among the tables
For half an hour and, as summer comes on, smell
That masculine smell. Admit it: you smell like a chorus
Line kicks. Sure, the sheepfarmers,
Cowpokes, and cardhustlers laugh
And jeer, and what would Jesus in Gethsemane
Say if he could see you now? Actually,
Woodrow doesn't look so good
In a tutu, but don't let that bother you. You look
Tart as a teardrop on your mother's face. Betrayal?
Ask her. Ask the cardhustler with the queen
Of hearts up his sleeve, the cowpoke fingering
His holster, the sheepfarmer with wool stuck
In his zipper. Hell, ask Jesus with his twelve-
Man posse. Ask them all what it means
To be a man. If Jesus could walk about
Without underwear, you can trust your own tutu.
Listen, boy, a man's gotta wear
What a man's gotta wear. Amen. Tulle
And sweat. Sure, the daily laundry of social
Convention weighs lighter every day
And that detergent—Cheer, Joy?—it whitens every
Black T-shirt. In a hundred years,
You'll still look young and good, a boy
Among old men. And then your mother
Will smile on you and Woodrow will prance around you.
In two hundred years, you'll learn to trust
Yourself. Autumn comes on, too, and colors
The metallic leaves the deepest crimson known
To birds and bees, so deep and ideal that no man

Can tell they've changed at all. Each leaf,
When it finally falls, falls for you. Check the mirror,
Boy: you and all the stubbled, confused
faces. What do you have to prove?
La guerre est l'amore, mon ami, et l'amore est la guerre.
All the tutu says is *please*. There is
No winter here. It's always spring.
Wipe your brow, belly up to the bar, order
A whiskey, and invite every man in the room
To take a shot with you and turn a turn. You know
As well as they do that when John Wayne finally
Rides off into that great pink sunset—no matter
What he's done or hasn't done—he sits tall
In the saddle and his horse's head is held high.

Laura Moe

Home Front

Memory slips like a tiny rocket
Off course from its mother
Ship. Old memories jump to attention
Like draft notices and a Glenn Miller song,
And it's the cat's pajamas,
Because we lived like there was no yesterday
And chanted, Don't Sit Under the Apple Tree
With Anyone Else But Me, like an anthem,
And Rita Hayworth's legs were
monuments of freedom.
We danced a blue jitterbug like the light fantastic
and were as carefree as sages.
Nights are now numbing cold,
Hair grows thinner, what's left glistens silver.
Thoughts of what we will miss
Boss us around like the taste of fishy water.
Old memories should be erased, given a clean plate
So Harold can sleep at night.
But old memories never really fade, do they?
They brighten, become colorized,
Like one of Ted Turner's movies.
We danced the war to end all wars, our feet plundered
The hardwood like bullets.
Laura wasn't born yet,
But she will remember it all and write a screenplay
And fill it with a thousand bombshells.
I'll program my cell phone to record yesterday's dialogues.
Elle a un joli cul, oui?
Street lights shouted as Rita walked by,
and the sidewalk hummed its approval,
and I remember it all like it was happening right now.

Leslie Monsour

Macbeth in Hell

Life is like a candle, flesh of wax,
soul of string, a higher power to light
its flame. Ignited, the candle's life is brief.
(The dripless ones are popular in Phoenix.)
A graceful amber flicker licks the air
And seasons it with vague, sweet promises;
The lip is tender at the melting point;
The taper rises, silent as a tree.
Extinguished on the tongue it tastes of ash —
A graphic, feathered flavor of indifference.

Luís Salinas haunts the Pedregal.
No vague, sweet promises hang in the air.
Volcanoes aren't erupting anywhere;
But picadors on tiptoe cross the ring.
The sand is soft, so soft, it rots their feet.

Après moi le déluge, pass the *crudités*.
The folding chairs of passion have collapsed —
They're almost as reliable as the Sphinx.
It's time to dance across the dome of heaven.

Milady likes to wear her hair in braids —
Tomorrow she'll go on an arduous journey
To view plump orphans toiling in the rain.
They seem to be perspiring inside out.
Vaya con diós, mi vida; vaya con diós, mi amor.
The woodpeckers keep corporate bank accounts.
The candle drips to tell us how its life is spent.

JIM NATAL

Borderline

Mexico is bleeding people.
I am opening the sky for them.
Some smell like ochre earth.
Some have skin rough as mongrel paws.
Others, wispy as clouds, refract light.
A few speak only in breezes.
I can taste the fires
in the kitchens they left behind.
The cold matches in my mouth
make a dried insect rattle.

Martín crossed near Patagonia, Arizona.
I did not open the sky for him.
Instead, I parted the river.
I walk along its banks waiting
for ocotillo to bloom; the manzanita
has such red branches . . . even now.
Only a *pendejo* or a *bruja* can see
beyond the flowers. Their petals
are so large they hide us from *la migra*.

You know what they always say:
"*El viento sobre la tierra tumba muertos.*"
Ah, yes, the land's remorseless wind
does blow away the dead.
Sunshine spills melancholy
as Martín collects rattlesnakes
and puts them in his pockets.
Puma won't sit beside him
when they stop for water—
he will stand only, tell his stories
from a distance, speak of neon cities
where it will rain
sticky money on them all.

Their haggard map points the way
to intersections with no corners.
But that's the way it is
once you pass *la linea*.
The gash is 2,000 miles long
and all the barbed wire in the world
cannot close the wound.

Geezz

Satan eats the wings of Angels with Tabasco sauce
as lesbians lick the plate clean of tuna.
It's my friend Lucifer who has three friends named Tuna,
they smoke a lot of marijuana so they must buy insane amounts of soap.
Chaleco Salvavidas Debajo de su Asiento.
They used to call each other cunt swabs during hockey practice
and in three days they will smoke imported cigarettes that
will have arrived the day after today.
Lucifer demonstrated how his penis can drill a thick hole through a sap tree,
Bianca the Bull noticed a lot of sap on his unit after the magnificent drilling
and the tree said, "that's the only thing I've known to be harder than me."
Actually Lucifer has five friends named Tuna
and one ate a bowl of gumption at the sock hop on 3rd avenue.
Everyone's ears twinkled with excitement about free
samples of K-Y jelly flavored cereal.
The prostituting cotton swabs of anger
pole danced on the Q-tips while
Norville Tampaxson frantically moved his hand
inside his front pocket in Cash-Wize Foods.
My sweet choir hymns, I love to sing them in the corridors of my plaid sheets,
I am two peanuts draped over a blanket of milk.
I spied someone shoving candy corn in my dogs nostrils; she forced 'em
out with a loud puff of snot and I licked their white tips.
These beautiful waxy candies smelt of divine pug,
permanently confined to a wheeled cart by nubby hind legs.
And what a tampon-refic morning it was,
Bianca wore flippin' floppers while fuckin' rockers.
With a kiddy pool of fourteen tuna
mackerels, smackin' lips of the
lower half.

EVE NICHOLAS

Playground

Children are hummingbirds
with voices of blurred wings.

Some throw stones, some fly
like jet liners, arms piercing the short sky.

They feel safest when lulled
in the scoop and rise of rubber swings

toes pointed like birds
converging on branches, pushed from behind,

a form of love
they rarely find at home.

They feel safest when drowning
in the tall weeds near the playground fence,

Bayville, New Jersey,
where boys with their hands jammed in their pockets

and girls with their mothers' stolen rouge
purse their lips like movie stars,

sing *Na-na-na-na-na*
then laugh with their ankles dipped

in the playground mud, its sodden brown grass.
The need for hiding

has run one girl, Lydia, beyond the fence.
She kneels at the foot of a parked car,

her knees pulled like weights to the ground,
her body pressed against the blue street.

There, Evie will find her
hiding within the sewer's grin.

She'll kneel at her side
practicing the childhood art of hiding,

the need to disappear
in the cement sewer of their untouched lives.

They will know each other's hands, the scars
on their knees

and they'll wait each day from September through June
as the sun dries the windshields

as waves of rain become songbirds of leaving.
In the gutters they'll stay, riding the tides

as if water could save them
as if rain could be tender against their skin,

deep in the spit-filled rain,
lips pursed, arms piercing the short blue sky.

SHAROSE NIEDELMAN

Finger Shadow

Shadows lurk outside
    the blown curtain
    of childhood's room

Though my shadow sleeps in a tree,
    she signs her name on every leaf

One sudden roar of frogs,
    chaotic dreams of prickly cactus, palm fronds
    jab my middle finger
    Gazing in the heat of a melting summer it drips
    And drips coolness on skin
    Succulent flavor of vanilla peach
    I walk by the aroma of Bronx Grandmothers

That mystical scent reminds me of seltzer blended egg cremes
And Tonya's rickety blue house with the alley gate
    where we fled as quickly as we arrived
    where we went through puberty during the mid '70s in Canoga Park, California

It wasn't my middle finger

I am humbled after a worthy day of living
Breath is the bomb, You are the bomb
We posed for a photograph that never appeared once taken
    Shadows   lurk   Shadows   lurk

Be careful the kinder
Shrieked the spinning crone of lost paradise
    she signs her name on every leaf
As I listen with my ring finger
My shadow eats wild midnight feasts of firelight

    burning curtains

Yiyo sings to stars as careening prayers
Her songs to sojourn the solar Earth,
welcome along backroads
a galactic suitcase of peacock feathers

Telepathic messages I do not know I do not know exist they not
a little piece of magic remained in the recipe

La pastille de menthe forte—a macher
The shell nestles the corner window,
the stone skirts the sunlit ledge

Where my finger traces and shadow lingers.

Jamie O'Halloran

Forty Nights

The sea of your hair parts to a Canaan
    I cannot imagine. The promised land
        Swims on your head. Milk blares from your eyes.

The leeks of your hair perfume a Canaan
    I can imagine. Reek of honey cradles
        Your scratchy chin.

If you lived in the land of *leche y miel* , above
    Your fine temples you would paint
        Figurative leaf-framed pictures and loathe

French philosophy. Whose land is this anyway?
    Whose promise for keeping?
        How good to know so little

Leaving me clear
    To build, anyway I can, you.
        In this fabricated future

You will blot smudgy
Moon from night to lighten
        Sleepless dark under my eyes.

Jamela feels your teeth, pull
    Of the small beard beneath your lip
        When a word's lost, thinking

Your way to its name.
    Your laptop smiles at me, not the mouth
        Of clay your big nothings sludge through.

I would make your hands epaulettes
    Raising my shoulders through the ranks
        Past the snobby barn of your parents.

O, comb the manna from your hair,
    Wandering one! Go down, Moses,
        Let me go.

ERIN O'KEEFFE

"Love is"

your
turbo smokin' 400 horse mega power plant
ramming my road like acid mouthwash
your premium grade Quaker State
on my quivering flesh
my thighs spontaneously combust
I smell your pistons thrust synthetic fuel
through dark, empty chambers
my skin red as blood-spattered leather
in Bonnie and Clyde's '34 Ford.

Because love can fizzle like an impotent spark plug
I'll pour my obsession into the redwood hot tub deck
wrassle them planks under the circular saw
cursin' 'em straight and smooth.

Pan Dulce, you are the deconstructionistic minimalist
of Nietzche's hungry desire.
His contritious wet dreams of Überman and cordless drills
no match for your full bore stroking dual cams.

So heroically painful, your bodysuit tattoo of geisha floating on carp
in a pool of margaritas.
Men, heads shaved and nipples pierced,
did you in the dark with a rusty nail.
You never complained.

Danke schoen, liebschin.

Mija, I may win the lottery and sweep you up in serial-numbered arms

or I may find you on blocks in the dusty backlot of a Tijuana bodego,
your perfumed headlights weeping with rust.

I can walk away or mambo on your radiant fins.

Straining through duct tape, you stroke my neck with frayed wires
and flaccid cables.
I fondle your hoses and pray you still remember
the sweetness of summers to which I surrender.

ASHLEE OWENS

What are you about?

Day goes by like a vicious wind
When I was the vicious one that day
The wind whistles through my ear
Sniffing the wetness
Feeling the coldness bubbling in my hand
The smoky dryness traveling through my mouth
Imagining it even though I can't see it.
The wind is visible, not able to feel,
But you can hear through your nose and taste through your mouth.

Casper lives in the haunted Taj Mahal
But if you can't see the Taj Mahal, how is it haunted?

Tears come out my nose and up my face
Into my eyes to keep them moist.

Man, I heard you were the soothsayer from Rome
Because you're smooth to soothe me to whistle false ways
It seems to me the only way for you to understand this method
Is to make an "O" with your lips.

The jumping clouds of greyness
Filled with rain and snow
We sank into a cloud
Filled with fire and hatred,
Then became hot, bloody stones.
This moment, right now, you will
Raise us above that cloud.

Next month, next year, I will destroy the soothsayer
For making the wind whistle false ways
And time will guide him to a dimension
That never existed
Y nunca se fue.
But I have to move on and give the soothsayer a chance.
Even wind has to breathe,
And even though you can't see the wind,
You can feel it whistling in your ear.

CARLA PANCIERI

Morning Bells are Ringing

An elbow is a date,
says Jeanne Kelly.
The concierge enjoys speaking French
to our breasts and laughing
but, through his raucous mime, he's made us understand
that New Year's Eve in Paris is for couples
and we aren't one. Well, we are a couple
of tourists who can't celebrate the New Year
because certain body parts have no one attached to them.
We're on our third day straight of salty ham
in restaurants where cigarette smoke overwhelms
expensive perfume. Notre Dame's holy water
is as cold as bed sheets in winter and someone
cropped the Mona Lisa to the size of an album cover.
Over the hum and clang of Metro trains,
Jeanne and Who, Me Homebody? sing
the only French they know: *Frere Jacques, frere Jacques,*
dormez vous? dormez vous? (They make up the next part).
At least Homebody isn't tone deaf.
Versailles treats us like peasants
so we spend the day as topiary (she's a tree cut like a poodle,
I'm a misplaced giraffe).
Italy has its pigeons, plus its hands are always on you.
From the top of the Eiffel Tower, we listen through fog
for city lights and roof tops.
"I could've stayed home for this," says a man from San Francisco.
The stone arch of homesickness expands in my rib cage.
The New Year signals the end for us.
We will wish one another Bony Annie.
We will revisit this place we'll never return to.
The concierge hands out paper cups for the champagne
and dances with our breasts.

JACKIE PETTO

The Graveyard Shift

Our kitchen table is a graveyard.
Skeletons die to speak.
Your hair lightens with gray
as your voice turns to gravel,
right in front of your untouched breakfast.
Your hands hold the texture of decay.

Did you take your pills? Do you
swallow them hard? Is your throat
bleeding?

I can smell your tits rotting from here.

The blue of your eyes tastes like cream cheese,
like oceans in Winter,
and a whale, I'm sure, still swims
beneath your clothes and skin.
It sings like Gloria Gaynor at the Apollo:
"I will survive."

Your voice is a cartoon bird's
shot while in flight (a sudden denouement)
just because your body can follow a shallow pitch in death.

The young daughter of old age
bites into her bagel,
teeth grinding the bread bones,
tongue mashing the white cheese skin
and the pulpy red jelly;
I reach over and bite into you, Mom.

I chew your skin and swallow.
I cough up hair and bone.
Your Bobbie Girl is full now.
I'll hide in the basement until my black dress
comes back from the dry cleaner.
(We'll choose the saddest color wood, Dad swears.)

My Mother is a living skeleton
and I am slowly killing her.

The young eat the old.

My bagel says I should let this go.
A bird sings out of tune, stops,
and my Mother asks me how I've been doing.

Sundays

Tyranny is a yellow flame, ha!
The blue center of its heat
brings a chill to my bones;
and the taste of other people's power
is a violent burning spice.

Don't think tyranny means the state!
Think of Great Aunt Ethel
on 92nd and Broadway,
how she tormented her younger sister,
Anna: The flame is too high the flame is
too low. Boiling an egg is an exact science,
isn't it? Anna burns, silent. No, she thinks,
the height of a flame is an intuitive measure,
and its icy blue hardens the yolk.

Miss Fafufnik, a visiting child from the Island
drinks milk at the kitchen table.
New York City is outside the window,
a clanking music box of insults.
She falls 19 floors
in her mind's eye
to reach a little park
with illegitimate trees.

Someday, Grandma's sisters will direct
traffic from the top of the Empire State building.
They will wear neon gloves of apology
and point to a revolution of forgiveness
just beyond gridlock.

Oh, the pies, the strawberry-rhubarb!
The kettle calls teaeeeeee
but nobody hears it while arguing.
Not only Grandmother, the innocent baker,
is deaf. Tyranny doesn't hear a word either,
and persists in her burning.

NORINE RADAIKAN

Child of Science
"Earth of Air, Spirit of Mind"

Science is a pyramid of bricks that reach unreality
The bricks feel cold, icy through our gaze
Pythagoras states numbers are reality in Greek

Science is more like a triangle of stone
That dissolves into the duality of Gemini
Like the familiar becoming estranged from itself

Like the uncanny air becomes a nuisance
When sun sets at dawn

The dark twin grounded to earth threatens to fly away
While the light twin with his baton becomes
Tomorrow their mother will return with Pythagoras
To make them whole again

The stone wall behind them is to the right of the celestial pyramid
Their mother will not be happy about their apparent indifference to theorem

CHARLES RAMMELKAMP

Ruminations of the Caged Beast

I woke up this morning a caged tiger.
But I'd read Kafka and Roth and I didn't feel so odd, transformed feline.
Like the gray area between taste and smell,
you can hear how it feels, rough as a cat's tongue
lapping up odorless gas, the foul-smelling flatulence
Gary Hirsch continually emitted in Civics class back
at Glen Cove Junior High. But it wasn't Gary. It was his sister, Jeanne.
Under the street lamps I watched her undress behind sheer curtains,
one item at a time until she was completely clothed.
Yo, dude, I have a boyfriend but I don't know his name, Jeanne said,
carelessly tossing the poison darts of jealousy into my heart,
causing my cries of envy precisely because my sorrow lurked behind my eyes,
thus driving me to the total despair of fey ballerinas and callow comedians.
So I held my breath for three hours and twenty-four minutes just to teach her a lesson.
Poor Charlie told himself to breathe again when the last bell had rung and school was over,
knowing that one day soon he will smell only aromatic perfume,
erotic odors and hairy fragrances from some time in the long ago future.
For only when you smell your own death does the bouquet of quintessence finally emerge.
Car Dieu a aimé si le monde qu'il a donné son seulement fils,
and that crucifix stretching its arms to embrace you smiles so fetchingly.
But still I'm prowling around my cage, ready to roar.

Diane Raptosh

Ears, An Essay

August and self-possessed as a pair of galaxies,
even the cauliflower ears that boxers get. Siamese
fighting fish eavesdrop on nearby duels to find
who wins. All we can see of the sky

belongs to the past; birds and gills and oceans
underfoot were once the lobes of a star. The ear
will bend the way Einstein figured space could
pinch its way back to black holes. Listen:

That ringing high behind the nose is the sound
of the mind at work. We fear what we know.
The thinking ear can single out twelve qualities
of sin. Fire roars back like a stubborn lion

or a favorite question. Why even unzip
if you can't hear the sound? The ear hole
grows into its flap, or pinna. From the Latin
growing toward. This is why things

must be understood backward and lived
the other way around. Never put anything in the ear
smaller than your left elbow. The steadied
listener will hear that shifty particle, the spinning

nothing. In one ear, and boom, your molecules
and mine are drifting off our skin. We blend in
to each other, open bottles of attar of roses. I smudge
the stuff along my ear tips, temples, and the backs

of my knees—a warrior painting herself
in scent. Gravity finally will pull us
toward a common center, those half-moon
labyrinth canals in fellowship with one another

like a theater of wordless people rallied
around digital noise. Memory keeps
a home for objects and a round, gray flat
mapped out for spatial affairs. The finest

streamlined body has no use for ears, the Siamese
fish suggests—flame-ripe and stately as a murk
of stars and gas, picking up on blue bygones,
lip-synching shades of being under siege.

R. FLOWERS RIVERA

Cris de Coeur

Emergency is the normal state of the body in love. Allegedly
Natty people dine nightly on meals of heart, lungs, brain.

Blinding white sheets, a noisome coldness, assaults my sense of smell,
And the clink of the surgical instrument twangs like metal on my tongue.

Lilith reluctantly leaves purgatory to tell me to lie still. Remonstrances and
Gainsayers abound; both sensa and viscera need rest. Constant rest.

Do formal rules of etiquette apply when eating internal organs?
I'd just as soon eat my heart out as cut out another's.

Hurtful words arrest hearts, constrict breathing, cause headaches:
"I remember you when you wasn't, and still ain't."

This dirgeful orison of death signals a genesis, I abscond
Into this place between heaven and hell—limbo.

Dossing down with a plebeian,
Nasty Rock swaggers away from the encounter

And, for the nonce, will no longer equate good sex with good love
Or confuse a muss of orbs with dusky stars.

Relationships never die in stages, but failing organs do.
No pienso en nada más excepto la pirámide del Sol y la Luna y las Estrellas.

Let heart and lung and brain say *amen*
As this corpse and its folderols are committed once again to earth.

LEE ROSSI

"The Vulture Knows"

I'm a ghost. Sorry,
what I meant to say is,
I'm Lord of Hosts,
and, as such, smell
like a stinkbug, taste
like tobacco, flame
like a firefly, cackle
like dry brush, and caress
your tongue like a peach's
crushed velour. But
you can call me Chick.
You remember how
the crushed rosemary
on your mother's fingers
tasted like lightning.
Kennedy was President
and Berlin a place
surrounded by wasps.
By tanks. But what if
I'm not the Lord, and
what I said was Hostess,
not Hosts (an error
in transcription)—
cream-filled cupcakes
and Twinkies. The red light
of civilization depends
on getting this exactly right,
oder? Weißt der Geier,
as my West German friends
used to say, whatever
they meant. How we loved to fly
like sparrows from one side
of the Wall to the other,
while the East Germans
sat in their guard towers,
benevolent, gently smiling
vultures. If you're still
reading, I'm sure you've

realized that the speaker
is not a messenger
of God's honest truth.
Doubtless he will spend
part of eternity
chewing baseballs for the
taste of horsehide. A goblin's
life for me, then, its
exquisite dastardy.
Better a medium oven
in hell, than the deep freeze
of inhibition. Or maybe not.
My cat, an avatar
of the Egyptian god
Osiris, smiles and says,
"Don't worry, kid,"
the ghost of wild tobacco
rising from his fur
like hillsides wet with fire.

Kathleen Roxby

The Tree Harp's Song

The tree harp is out of tune
For monkeys are tone deaf.
They've tuned it for a red wind
That tastes of sand and summers lost
Amid the salt fields of Thailand
When Mr. John was young.
The ice hot sun then . . . burned
The sloughed off acrid skin.
Monkeys played so beautifully,
Composing new songs each day—
Sweet melody filled the air.
"My mama don't raise
no dumb babies"
Slaps you upside your head.
The red wind of memory
Guts your soul like wet leaves.
You will walk the sky down,
Spit lava at the sea
As Milly, the alter-self of me,
Slips the deep-carved deskfront.
The tree, not amused, moans—
Ne me quitte pas.
Ne me quitte pas.

LYNN SCHMEIDLER

My Muses Sit Upon Uncomfortable Chairs

Writing with children playing downstairs
is like whipping meringue with a baby spoon.
          Piercing squeals seeking limits in teenage reproach.
From above I smell the texture of mutiny,
my nose stings with its cracked lip warning.
          The babysitter, flipping elbow-long hair over
          her shoulder, is reliable as a weather report.
I must learn to clamp my head and loosen my heart.

The restless computer screen blinks off
then quivers, rolls its eyes
and reveals full-tongued lettering in pale irises.
          Like B movies, the afternoons will replay
          with the same scraps of screams and heavy footfalls
invading from beneath the too-large crack under the door.
          One sitter will morph into the next,
          these girls whose eggs have only just begun to fall,
          who could be my eldest children, who I need to love my children.
          They enter the house amidst desperate protests, then
          leave in tornadoes of unfulfilled needs.

If I store my ideas all week in my cheeks
          like a squirrel,
then images will flow from tingling fingertips to type-set truths.
The universe will sigh.
Meanwhile, my muses sit
upon uncomfortable chairs with little back
support, sorting the whirlwind in my mind.
They feed on chocolates
          pirated from a five year-old's birthday loot,
whispering wet secrets in my head.

*

A glob of dry paint on the wall, a blot of
                                    purple earwax on a child's lobe,
returns me to primeval times when
        I was an ape intent upon grooming,
                eating bugs off my family's fur.

                                    *

Daylight behind curtains crumbles old and faint.
Down the hill, a neighbor's chimney wafts
smoke through cracks in my window frame.
        A knock on the door and Jonah appears, ancient
globe under small arm, pointing to
                        Madagascar, "Are you allergic to lemurs?" he demands.
    "Mommy!"   Eva crosses the threshold of my sacred space,
    "Jonah says I don't have a pee-pee!"
        All over her face mortification melts
                like a warm ice-cream sandwich.

                                    Basta Cosi!

When I was their age, my mother
sat with us at the kitchen table gluing
felt and pom-poms on old coffee cans.
Because we all ate the same thing
at dinnertime, we had a healthy family life.
Now petrified memories of my childhood stick
            to the roof of my mouth.

                                    *

Flying over my desk through gossamer curtains,
I alight on an heirloom pink canopy bed.
        The girl I was will become a young woman
            reading poems naked with mud-masked face.
She'll grow to spend evenings searching
                in the grays and blacks of moving fonts.
                    She has found happiness, but doesn't know this yet.

*

Once family
meant naiveté disguised in fat fortune.
So I scuba dive into the deepening past
and fish out rusting hulks
of obligation and resentment. Guilt
          startled children cower in a thunderstorm,
          plunge under beds, leaving dwarf mud prints—
          sole proof of having played,
as the words on my screen call
out from their posts on
                    the glaring front lawn of fantasy.

PEARL STEIN SELINSKY

The Road to Sisterhood is Seldom Straight

They are sisters, a stork and a swan.
The swan could out-fly the stork.
The white of feathers seen against the sky is matched only by the clouds.
As I finger my beloved's chest, I touch childhood's teddy bear.
Like beans heating on a stove, his scent guides me home.
Each swish of tires against snow sounds a knell—Sound on, soft bell.
To tongue summer's fruit again is the wish of every spring.
How rash-measle-red my sister's voice as she splotches everything I do.
She is not Scarlett, nor from Tara's hill.
It is the stork that flies; the swan never does.
I need my sister, seek her advice for everything I do.
She makes me feel like such a *jerk*.
Because I love a man, no woman ever will be my friend.
"Ay, ay," Grandma told me, "it's all the same, garbage in and out."
The fragrant blooms of youth are seldom smelled in age
My longing dwells in the icy halls of hell.
My sister will scrub my beloved's back.
She thinks that Tubby doesn't know the way she feels.
The two will be so closely bound, no love will ever come between.
It is a slippery knot that binds.
My gift of Einstein's picture is the bottom line.
Aunque yo amo mi hermana, me vale mas tus labias.
"It is now," the swift hawk said, "and now is when we two must fly,"
and so born aloft, light echoes lake and sky.

Evie Shockley

News

　　　　We look up into that vast ocean of moody
gases, hoping for news. Some days the clouds
are merciless pugilists, beating each other
dark gray and blue, threatening to drown us
in anger. *Il pleure dans mon coeur, comme il pleut*
sur la ville—we ought to know better.
　　　　　　　　　　　　　　　　　　　I've
seen a flock of birds rocking back and forth
on the wind like a collective kite, anchored
to my eyes by a thick string of desire, their cries
guttural. Unlike us, the blackbirds know
where they're going.
　　　　　　　　　　　Some days the sun slips
through the clouds like a sonata. Some days
the sky serves sun like hot, yellow joy pie,
steaming from the oven, and we feast until
our bellies are full.
　　　　　　　　　　Imani, who's good at this,
swears the sky in Vancouver is farther away
than here in North Carolina, where its blue
is practically domestic.
　　　　　　　　　　　We will wish we
hadn't counted on the stars.
　　　　　　　　　　　　　　The blackbirds
have no idea where they're going, but unlike
us they don't make a fuss about it.
　　　　　　　　　　　　　　Cutie knows
she's got the moon to thank for that midnight
spent in the melted ebony of the sea, when
the difference between swimming and flying
disappeared. Warmer water floated above cool
currents, like the smell of baking cornbread
rides the rose-musk scent of my mother's
perfume.
　　　　　　　We can't bear to be told no.
　　　　　　　　　　　　　　　　　　Some
days the sky is a blank slate, and we scribble
and sketch all over it. But our doodlings are

125

dreams, not signs, and taste as flat as a glass
of soda four days old.
                              We were all born under
the sign of hootchie-cootchie, the stars in blissed-
out disarray, and we act like it. The zodiac is
as shifty as scripture.
                              It snowed all spring
in Vermont that year, because I was there.
The rough thumb of loneliness pressed down
on me like that gray-white sky, and only the
mountaintops could break free.
                                        Some days
the heavens look like something the cat drug
in: some mangled catch of birds, clouds, stars,
and stale dreams, all threatening to rain.

Ann Silsbee

See A Penny, Pick It Up

The moon's a coin, light money of luck,
so Aunt Hazel would say. *Pluck it*
from the sky, roll it in your fingers.
Feel its bony knurls, raised glyphs
from an old-time language a woman
has to understand. It's her dowry.

I want my coin to buy poverty,
Aunt Hazel's kind, that has a need
to listen, desire to smell the mood
of river water, hunger to breathe in
the helixed wind of moon music.
I want to dare to ride its whorls.

Just think what Armstrong risked,
wading that dust-shoaled lava flow
of basalt dark, *Mare Tranquillitatis.*
Imagine Cortez, gazing on the Pacific,
guessing this must be the finialed
edge of the world, this other sea
the blood of earth which links us all.
Cool kid! your brothers shouted,
as you toed the verge of your first
twenty-foot dive. And your mother,
in the very blood-wrack of your birth
had to go on and push you through.

I want Aunt Hazel's kind of mind-
calm, round window like a moon
through which she'd peer at a future
hunkered down, a bird of prey
pruning his gloomy talons, quonking
his beak against the rind. Chance?
It was water to Aunt Hazel, a river
she paddled all the time. The trick's
to catch the bird not looking your way,
make him take wing, not let his sour
croaking scare you. Go with him, jump—
though ground is slippery with maybe,

good luck so porous night can't enter,
night so thick even a moon can't budge,
however she weeps those silver tears,
her face a cat's without ears, a window
chary of secrets. *O ye of little faith,*
you hear her say, *will you go for yes?*

Aunt Hazel, too: *Pick the penny up!*
You have to suck the tart-sweet juice
from that white grape of promise,
spit the seeds into black nothing.
Then when earth thickens back to dark,
some shard of light is sure to sprout.

ANNE SILVER

It's All Refuse

My life is a dumpster of complaints.
When people see me
they contribute a can of kvetch.
Sad coffee grinds pepper the sulphuric yolks.
My pits reek of rotten oranges.
My sides are thumped daily with putrefied sausages.
I taste decomposed melon rind
and run my hands along congealed Crisco in my braids
Hearing gripes about lack of money
tastes like motor oil sliding into my ears.
I got a B when I earned an A
from Mrs. Parker at Bagley Elementary in Detroit.
Do I gripe about it for the rest of my life?
I actually like living in an alley.
Oaxacans bicycling to work
toss non-recyclables on top of my head.
Taggers spray my sides
and I am percussive when the occasional guava
falls on my closed lid.
As if I give a flying fig about cheating spouses,
the care of somebody's old lady they never even liked.
Because life is short and so is the arc of the garbage truck's arm
lifting and emptying my insides.
Meow meow meow needs no translation.
Ah, the fine whine of memory.
Even years after my mother died,
I can recite all the names of those folks
who betrayed or let her down.
She spooned dead hope into my little ears.
My skull stretched into a wastebasket.
As a teen a trash can.
Old Hi Ho Dented Sides, I became the familial confessional.
I was groomed to service a whole apartment house of offal.
The decoupaged laments
the bondage of clerking at the Safeway,
deadbeat dads,
the sting of gonorrhea
plaster my floor, ceiling, walls.

I digest others' worries
so I can recall my mother's lullabies.
Buruch ata Adonai
The rain keeps me company.
The winter brings no grass clippings.
Without me, garbage would carpet the ground.

RENEE SIMMS

The Death of Soul, a Remix

I've decided to marry a treble clef or break beat
men, sex, music are that intertwined in my life
me and my future husband will speak exclusively in song lyrics
or island patois, pidgin, *rien que Anglais*, unless it's rhythmic
like: you're jinglin' baby/go 'head baby
you're jinglin' baby/go 'head baby

I blame this alchemy of men and music on my childhood
which rocked with tambourine shakes, doo-wop harmony
and in every other house lived a slick-pretty man who could sing.

Men with bass-guitar voices, men inside pyramid homes, men
driving Cadillacs glossed by the moon. How could I not be
peculiar? Post-Motown Detroit, air still ripe with miracles
and temptations and me with wild, flapping feelings
between my nine year old thighs.

Then 1977, he arrived.

He was guitar riffs and wanton falsetto, everything I felt
but could not express, only knew it when I heard it
like when his anthem spun soft and wet on FM radio.

My best friend's daddy, who sang backup, didn't like him.

Pornographic, her daddy said. The devil, Mama would say
but what did they know? My girlfriend's daddy kept
women vacant as Smokey Robinson's house and
Motown was dead at the edge of a continent—
the pious heel-spins by suited men, clichés
we no longer used.

I tape-recorded my love's voice, carried scrolled parchments
with his songs, memorized his impish face. He was what it
meant to be young and hot, to be distilled between
the rub of bricks, Funk and your parent's social movements.
He was North American royalty, was cravings
unsheathed, the center of a flower,
seduction as a principle.

Nothing is permanent.
Not neighborhoods or soul music.

Even my history of lovers mimics staccato:
I've loved dozens of dark, polished men
who were abruptly gone

DAVID STARKEY

Poem to Beer

Like a bee on the tip of my tongue,
its tiny wings buzz.
Already my lids languish,
my inner anvil's muffled in velvet.
The sour smell finds its way
to my throat, cold aluminum
tingles my fingertips.
I taste the Elgar on the radio.

Gerald Locklin, you and I drank warm beer
in the public houses of Hull at noon.
Language, too, hummed
in The Star and Garter,
The Spurn Head Arms. The bitter
filled our mouths with words.
"Right, all right?" the bartender asked
as we stumbled into the bright
fist of afternoon closing time.
But rather than take a dive
we rose like martyrs above the streets.

Beer was our parachute.

Today, I awake from my nap queasy,
dreaming of dishwater.
Securus judicat orbis terrarum,
said St. Augustine as he conquered
the world with chatter, pious
and sober, the hem
of his robe winking the gold of lager.

MELISSA STEIN

Wings

i.
Blue dragonflies buzz me like warplanes.
Their wings taste of rock candy,
smell like cellophane, hum
like a dentist's drill. I want it
in my palms, that isinglass, I want it
rooted to my bones. I want right-angled
flight. Their only cargo's that long body, the burden
of flight itself—I had it once. The plank
gave way; the bridge was tall; the wind
was stiff. And I resigned. Because it was over
I was quite safe. When water came up
like asphalt I barely splashed. That was it.
I still feel that wind and *the ache*
in my shoulder blades for want of wings.
I still feel height and the clarity of it.

ii.
The drowned women in my dreams
have me at last; weed-strung hair,
weighted feet. Hope bloats:
I'll carry them home, numb limbs
and all, tuck them into my sound
sheets. Comb their snarled hair
to silk. Stir them soup. Stoke
the wood stove. And sing, sing
lu lu lulu lu, hush-a-bye and
tie a yellow ribbon and *this train*
don't pull no sleepers. Till they're dreaming
in their soggy beds, dreaming of me, parched
field of brushfire grasses, bleached gold
and dangerous. Wave after wave
of heat, wave after wave of bodies
colliding in midair, torn wings still
better than ours, better than ours.

MICHAEL BERNARD SYKES

The Trees were Whispering

Madame's tongue, a caustic simoom.
Madame's heart, an arctic tempest coveting fire.
Anointing you with love, she hated you.
You were not him.
Caressing with numb hands, seeking through cataracts
tasting vinegar in the sugar.
Rancid bouquets sting the nose as sober lyrics wrangle surdity
Madame's enmitous speech singed the ears' palate
Phyllis, Phyllis Hyman. Pittsburgh, PA.
She loved you truly, because you were not him.
I was told there was no Santa.
I would leave him cookies and milk anyway
Madame wanted you to run to her. You couldn't, the haha was too wide.
Suicide is painless.
Madame's smiting mace nutured exile.
"Such a lovely corpse" I thought,
as she took wing into the wind.
Ironman's rust streaked down his face.
Madame will light here when she returns
tender talons embracing me.
Everyone will hear our silent song.
"Limpe para fora da dor, dança levemente ao sond da cor"*
The flowers' shed tears.
The trees whispered amongst themselves,
"A voice shattered on the concrete."

Simoom — a very hot and very dry Saharan wind that scorches everything
Enmitous — bitterness, hate
surdity — deafness
Haha — a moat or ditch used in defense

* *limpe para fora da dor, dança levemente ao sond da cor*—Wipe out the pain, dance softly to
the sound of color–Brazilian Portuguese. This is a line from a song by Milton Nascimento
and Andreas Vollenweider.

SUSAN TERRIS

When Pistachios Rain from the Sky

The Tuscan sky is like a deep inverted bowl.
Pistachios rain down from it and rattle on the roof.
As the dog growls in the tones of her lost lover,
she sees nuts spiral past windows,
smells their salty pink flesh.
Then she and the children run outside,
gather them in their aprons, split them with
their teeth as the dog tromps on the shells.

Dante, she thinks, may have been in Florence
on a day when pistachios rained from the sky.
They weren't pistachios, of course—
more like stones, small crystal-hearted geodes.
Dante could lead her, she thinks, away from stones
onto the 7th ledge where lust is removed
and fiery shades burn with tales of chastity.
Nessun maggior dolore . . . a disembodied voice

warns as the mirror shows her lover grown old.
Eyeing him, his beard and wild eye, she smashes
the mirror, sure he's brought more than
7 years of bad fortune. Brandishing shards,
she sends him and the children out where
it's raining stones. *The grass widow*, she says,
peering into a silvered triangle, *can dance
with the dog and make stones turn to diamonds.*

When the children come home again, leading
their children—eyes shining like pale diamonds—
she will welcome them. They'll spill their
bright young eyes into her apron and wait for her
to open them into the future. Then the mirror
will mend itself, and she, Dante and her lover,
the children, the dog, the stones will whirl
through flames of light into the bowl of the sky.

SUSAN THOMAS

Weather Report

This week is an obscene phone call.
The air's heavy breathing makes me sick.
It keeps me up at night with its stench
of freezing sweat, fugitive whispers and shrieks.
I hate the taste of the wind, how it paws at me
all day. I hate how the sky breaks, leering with
its one dim eye. My hands are screaming

for a chance to smack this week off the map.
They say Mohammad Ali could punch it to China.
But I say not enough; I want this week deported
to Mars, where they don't have any weather so
they lay out all day getting red. (Because of
the crimson dust they don't get an even tan.)
But textuality integrates semantic components

while monster bubbles of darkness roll
from nearby stellar nurseries and the Milky Way
suckles her newborns in fury. She needs a break
from the workload, packs it in for a week in Hawaii,
sipping Mai Tais with Big Mama, the fat queen of hula.

You know, next week won't be any better.
The mutagenic weather report calls
for tropical flurries with suicide bombers.
Il pleure sans raison dans ce coeur qui s'ecoeure.
The sky is faking its courage—
see it cover its eye with both hands?

LYNNE THOMPSON

Every Dog's Martini

We are the olives in every dog's martini
served from the hollow of a big, white bone.
The dogs smell of pepper and dew.
With them, we are upright as rugs.
To them, we are has-beens.
Without them, we are sorry shit-kickers.
In pity, they politely shed their coats
y alimentado los ocho pollos.[*]
To console them, I put lingerie in their bowls,
but the poodles hear my panties melting,
see how like roses they perish.
Everything they dream is a dream of Marrakech
or a nightmare in Tunisia in a Dizzy Gillespie war.

Our libertine conflict will end in some dog's pen
where she'll howl "Summertime" *a capella*
from the limb of a baby linden tree.
Tomorrow, all dogs will bark for the priests,
wolf down a hairy communion,
then stack the Tarot and deal the cards
while sucking olives from their blue martinis.

[*] *and feed them to eight chickens*

MADELINE TIGER

Open Stanzas

Stanza means *room*; *camera* means *room* (Italian)

A *stanza* has been, well, known as a little *room*
an Italian *camera*; the root of faith is in imagery,
you will proceed like a proverbial bull through
the tiny China shop of tin where horrors fall
and fall. They echo senseless on the cutting floor,
the scent is lily blood, *ordure,* aloe, dog, *citron,*

a sweating masquerade, *une soupe citrouille,* trompe
l'œil: grapevines draped in blinking lights *oh la
chaleur! Coq* that crows no hour crows all night,
cows browse the stubbled hill and low till dawn,
"doves" (dirty pigeons from *le pigeonnier*) coo
in the eaves and drop white shit on the cement floor.

No light. No room for doubt (or faith).
We kick the cat and pray and move toward a meal,
no walls, *Mouche! Mouche!* we call, and swat and
scratch and cover the trays to keep away whatever
clutters the air. The floor crawls; the hot wind howls.
The lines are prayers–for grace, a revelation,

where to dig the well, for green, for *zanman* (trees).
The bull is false, (*sotto voce*) really a paper bull or
a boy, or a song, in this imaginary place. Stand tall,
reach up, touch the hanging vines, the soft shine
of the singed leaves leaves a sudden pang of bitter
memory on the one line you may repeat. Repeat

after Marie, it's good to breeze past the enjambed
limb, *la jambe de cet arbre faux,* oh *ce faux pas.* Oh!
Mon taureau, tu me tiens fixée! I taste the fierce
burn of your eyes, no surprise to the Mad Tiger:
her animus outgrows the stanza lines and sings
Don't fence me in, a fancy way of saying *Let my*

people go, which doesn't mean leave me alone
with Ma Belle(M)argot (no cell phone here), nor
Shulamith of "raven hair," nor the first Madeleine
who towered over the Galilee (*Kinneret*, lyre-shaped)*
region and sea, that woman whom no stanza
could hold, no Book contain, like the Bull of Minos

unchained from fable. She roamed, could not maintain
her sweet power. Jerusalem bowed, then pressed her out
from between the lines, her stanza was marked, cut
and bled for errant ways. But Beauty lives, and love
sustains the line: *Wherever the gospel is preached
in the whole world, what she has done will be told*

*in memory of her (Mark*14:9) and her power to re-
ceive the world, to the hear the dove's wings, to see
stone move. Beware! For what you do not see will
come, a ghost roving in apocrypha and Gnostic history.

A stanza may leave little space for bull (the
shitty lies you pass off on the natives, all you horny
missionaries coming off the runway, in your two's
and three's–pink, pink.) Please
leave a line between, please
read: *Stand back*, the camera sees

your talking tongues, catches
your hot breath. Episcopalians resist
but eat their diocesan words (their feasts)
with Eucharist, the wine pours down
in dusty pools along the country road,

la route est rocailleuse, the bread is
too soon stale, it sticks in Mady's gorge,
le ris est dur, she chokes between the lines
behind la *barrière—ti moun san fanmi.*

Who holds the key
to this *Academie* will grow
beyond *la terre de son pays*, will farm
a territory, irrigate a hope
for world beyond the island world
pa se se moun andeyo yo ye

where *Créole* milk will flow
from axed fruit in Jacmel, along the beach,
the *cochon*-rooting beach, where we Marie *et moi*
dared plunge in
                    to our detritus-swirling sea, the sundown sea.

Au coucher du soleil, the skinny *chiens sauvages*
will scavenge like the bull who broke into my words
demanding open form.   Does every beast
(do we?) demand a little room to roam
to feel along the zigzag lines behind the walls
within the walls at home?

* *migdal/magdalen* means *tower*

A.K. Toney

No. #3 Big Blus

strangers r common as passions of mind
like being naked with blunt between lips
sight for sore iris
contact my foreskin with a grab and pull
fragrant sex inside mist of nose
screams of insatiable
palate flavored pear apart
tasted like i heard within yr wims
rode bus W. down Manchester, met Mia
and continued N. on Lincoln

iniquity is imagined such as yr brush of affection
. . . has wiped yr body like sky
my bad! . . .
a kiss would turn yr voice from sweet to loud
lil' tender look wet behind ears.

blu be water washing yr virginity as signed virgo
flying in right on time is too early not enough late
she whispered tattoos of hearts running down my thighs
and Fluffy Lavender became soft as April

This Loose Angle wind blows tears for Chi-town nomads reaching . . .
reflective globes turning yr image into somebody
though i am, she is, we r nobodys in your greeting
Una-fahamu, Wadada?
music read a book through conversation leaving
keep in touch memory, forgive us stranger . . .

WILLIAM TROWBRIDGE

High Performance, Low Mileage

I put on wings tips when my walk says
panel truck.
            My Porsche came with two ejection seats.
When I peel uphill, the g's get good, the smoke
smells bitter as historic Philadelphia,
white as Swedish tragedy.

I'll buy wing tips if you'll show me how
to drive.
            Uncle Shirley knows the Pope enough
to hear his nickname's Gearhead, that his wicked
speed-shift turns his game face slightly
Oriental.
            My cookie told me, "You're due
for a bit of the genuine Naugahyde,
Mr. Blight Nuts."
                        She had a great set
of belteds.
            Ergo almost then and there,
passion overhauled my gait, replaced
Joe Blow with a real Olympic hoofer.
                                    I'm lucky
migraines give us sharper views, lighter
heads; or was it just those hi-top Elijawans
bringing home all that gold, that downtown moxie?

Some rainy day, I'll start my engine like a gent,
drive careful instead of leasing Yugos.

Mein Sauerstoffzufuhr reicht nicht aus? Don't hold your breath, pal.
A Buick shift's got no position for the Hully Gully.

When I'm better, I'll tint my moon roof zebra.
                                    Then watch
those tires sing stardust, those Florsheims
shimmer into overdrive.

KATHRINE VARNES

First Marriage

Imagine his heart a bagel,
a blueberry bagel with onion spread
that smells like soap or rinsing agent. He says

*How do you know a word
that I don't know?* and his voice squeaks like
an arrow of indifference only Everyone,

even Harold Bloom, cares.
Bunnies start multiplying in my dreams;
I put a balloon in my skirt so it buoys up. I'm pregnant

every day for two years
but no baby arrives. I swallow pink
dots of the ellipsis. He says *Honeybear*.

No he doesn't. I don't
remember that. He says Mrs. HisName
and I'm all who the hell does she think she is?

And he says *blueberry blueberry
blueberry jam dontcha dontcha love me
for the man that I am?* And does a handstand

on the edge of a knife. And the knife
starts chattering like teeth and when I bite
into it, it tastes like butter. The circle of his heart

forms words that sound like
break me now, bite me now, bait me now, now
I fall into a sleeping. *Wie schöne stille träume!*

And when the bunnies turn
into strippers I call Hugh, tell him
Fire the piano player. I say *He's got*

blueberry stains all over
the ivory and my baby's teeth
are blue. My sweet baby's teeth are blue.

PAT VIERA

Vanilla is an Orchid

i crave the decadence of absinthe and toulouse lautrec
of dark skinned slaves accustomed to bitterness who
would rather die than cut cane from these chartreuse fields

i long for barns in those woods that smelled of yellow-eyed
owls and blonde-haired girls like theresa belzberg who had the sweetest
tits west of my mississippi

i remember the god of new world movement who brought her lover
a renaissance fisherman whose hands, delicate unlike the rest of him
would later write this story from memory

                    it starts with a poem to a far away woman:
your land begins and ends with the color of thunder
remarkable birds these prophets red as costa rican clay
tiny fire lanterns illuminate you
fragrant rhythm, a distant drum moves me there
barefoot the humid soil of nightfall
dance in your open blouse
persimmons bursting ripe orange with nostalgia
and spanish heart
recline for me, wet me your amber rum
naked in sweat, scandalous, you'll think. i ask again
ven, al fin que estamos solas amame, con fuego y calma amame
hands fluid, steady as rain unfasten me,
underwear cut at upper thigh designed for a penis
you like this sort of thing, it's why i choose you, every moment
a risk, and then you say "nowhere for you to live where i won't want you, mount me
now, daddy, i was born for this."

months pass, silent the fisherman's hands
still you remember those chartreuse fields
where the distance of life won't empty my hands of you
it will take years before anything grows there
i get up and look further, it saves me from this world

ALICIA VOGL SAENZ

Winter in Los Angeles

Late afternoon peeks through blinds
like a sealed letter held up to light.
Stairs lead me to you, each step a word
layered atop another, folded paper.
There is no second floor.
Footsteps creak through walls,
disturb our salty lips. Koi swim
in the courtyard, brush against underwater
plants, my fingers in your hair.
Vanilla ice cream, you whisper,
heavy as Rothko's blue.

A minute with you is as long
as a Thomas Mann sentence,
is a train ride up the Swiss Alps.
Thin air is easier to breathe.
You and I are as still as that train,
our motionless bodies of desire
too startled to say goodbye.
It is like when Thomas stood,
his back to Germany, eyes
on Santa Monica Bay,
remembered *parler français
c'est parler sans parler,
en quelque manière.*

You and I don't speak French.
Next week blue will smell
of New York in winter,
breath suspended
between buildings. This
afternoon Alika wears red
and winter in Los Angeles
is summer in December.
Your hand on my nape
reflects orange sky,
our words shudder, airplane
a second before take-off.

Cheryl D. S. Walker

Untitled

love pursues like rain chases
dirt off tasty sidewalks,
while books dance to jazz's soulful licks
and words light upon midnight's dew

"Escuchas unos discos," habla Cheryl,
as she fancies Utah within her reach
her love for him rests upon
the finality of never's ending

gazing upon his savoriness
she swallows softly to internalize his touch
and chews his sultry sonnets
to anger blatherskite gods

she listens for his coming and
despises the love he professes as it
stings like butterflies resting upon
green blades leaning

the Chicago winter's warmth elicits
spirited music of infinity
so I grasp oxygen with left hand
and carve it into onyx kissi stone

to give future's secret to Cheggy
to share today 'cuz I roll like that
just as jazz molds sound
into a sanctuary of solace

FRANK X WALKER

Birth Rights

She hibernates in the oven
In the back room.
The devil is hiding
Near the bathroom door.
His laughter echoes in the dark.
The smell of blood, brown
Is thick, bundled in white tissue
Unmasked by the vinegar in the air.
She is barely visible beneath her tears.
Little Jane Doe has refused her invitation
To Oil Mill Quarters, Rapides Parish
Alexandria, Louisiana.
He wasn't really laughing and we weren't
Really that far south.
Outside the fruit trees are budding
And the farmers are waiting out the frost.

"Pulling out ain't neva got nobody pregnant
whatcha mean you late?"
The hollow side of lust and sex
Is filled with empty promises.
True love is as permanent as first teeth.
A fetus crawled backwards through her umbilical cord
And aborted her would be father.
The X man witnessed it all.
In eight weeks they will regret their moment of pleasure,
Wrestle with fluorescent tongues
Take soy milk baths, together
And believe
Its never too soon to learn from your next mistake.
Yo siempre tengo cuidado.
For I have seen the toilet bleed
And sinners double down with the devil.

PAM WARD

The bullets in the road

The car dance ends with a bang.
Broken glass guitars my gut.
The engine coughs its one last smoke
it chokes on what my headlights swallow
I hear my slow spilled oil can breath
My hands can taste the heat.
And even Ford, in Detroit blue
just strikes his match and grins.
But cars don't dance and glass can't play a single note
It's me who life drives crazy.
My hooptie would not move one inch,
unless I twist the key.
You end up where you steer, my love,
those turn signals don't lie.
Even "Engine, Engine number nine"
could not trust its own track.
The smeared ink Thomas Guide of streets
can't lead you to the truth.
If red lights hadn't told me "go."
If yellows weren't so boring.
I'd roar, I'd stay completely lime,
I'm her on hairpin curves.
A license plate echoed her name
her last one screamed, "Revenge"
But winding roads and wounded hearts
will surely lead to wreckage.
No matter how you till your dirt
a fuel tank won't grow flowers.
But sometimes gas and melted grease
is better than a hand gun
"Les bon temps a rouller, my sweet,"
the fuel pump told the throttle.
"You end up where you steer, my love,
please do not ask us why."
The rearview mirrors of fate don't show
the bullets in the road.

MICHAEL WATERS

Wedding Party

Her parents arrive clean as newly-minted coins,
but Romanians have no relationship with money.
Her father smells like tobacco. Her mother smells like tobacco & lipstick.
Each spoons the air with a curled tongue
& eyes the grimy afternoon light in Queens.
Gypsy violins blare from taxis, familiar yet wrong
as her mother clasps her father's formal woolen sleeve,
rough as the industrial drizzle bleaching their lips.
Welcome Mr. & Mrs. Moscaliuc from Suceava
who appear less scrubbed in the airport parking lot.
Rock'n'roll home-schools the children of immigrants
who scrawl *bootylicious* on their girlfriends' thighs
to impress upper-management at KFC.
"Buna," her parents repeat, smiling at me,
the lascivious professor of cosmopolitan theory.
"Buna," I reply, sheepish as a dictator,
breaking birds on my scalp & leaping barricades.
Moosecock unlocks the orphanages!
Those blinking wards of state will tender my bedsores in 2029
& cleanse my Catholic marrow.
When I'm dead, you must call me Elizabeth.
Sa fiu mai mult, fiind doar jumatate?
Her parents' shoes begin to tap their impatience, raggedy laces
jabbering a plethora of directions
as the New World prepares its overture of abundance & sorrow.

M. Gwin Wheatley

En Durango, scorpions are king.

I've survived these long years drinking
only poison. My tongue tastes velvet warm
and I smell peaches, hear ants

walking and calling
the name of my lords—*Los alacraneros.*

Once I danced with hunters,
stirred hands in refuse
to find writhing ones, trophies for *las medicas.*

Scorpion venom can save your life,
and 'the life you save may be your own.'

San Jorge will protect you. The sharp
bite of wisdom will slap you back to frivolity,
pinch you from the precipice.

I might dance again.
I can only live clean waiting.

Con las picaduras del scorpion, el tiempo es oro.

KELLEY JEAN WHITE, MD

You are a river to our city

The trolley changes course
to mark your birthday.
Everyone eats Italian
ices on sizzling new tar.
Tongues buzz the color pink.
Mussolini salutes you from
his monumental horse.
It is Tahiti, we eat
Tahitian treat snowcones.
No, we use the syrups
to paint your nails.
They have grown long,
a symbol of your immortality.
Mon cheri, Mon amour, Toot Sweet.
In spring the little flowers bloom:
children wear red hats.

He ain't ashamed of nothing. *Sacre* Blue.
The dark hounds of indiscretion bark
up your tree. Tin cans dance attendance
on your priest. You bow
to his authority. Shriven. Me, Miss
Suicidal, will learn calm.
Pretentious sidewalks await
your expedition.
Honi sant qui mal sepanse.
Fire engines bow down
to you in homage.
The trolley crosses swords
with the crosstown bus.

JILL WILLIAMS

Bipolar (in 20 projects or less)

To be bipolar is like changing skins.
Ask Jake, the Rattlesnake. He knows the drill.
"Hiss off!" he'll cry and flap those scales like fins.
"You smell bodacious, man. Like Dollar Bill."
He's nuts, ya know. We're all pecans in drag.
So round and Jilly-Willy. *Quelle domage!*
The crescent moon of mental health's a hag
Whose only beauty lies in God's garage.
To be bipolar is a simple thing:
Like two and two makes chalk dust on the boards.
'Tis sweeter than the taste of vintage Sting.
Or speeches at Academy Awards.
Our snake of insight's in the grass, the creep.
Because it's dawn and children have to sleep.

KATHERINE WILLIAMS

Dream Date

The Day paints her nails red before slipping on
first one black fishnet stocking, then the other

she has a lot on her mind

desert wind teases her cloud hair
sunlight is the slip beneath her hem
her music the baying of wolves
taste of moon on her lips
with meadow's dew she dabs her wrist

her finish is so close she can hear evening
on the treetops through her fingertips

now that she's ready, she decides
that King Chango's in Peach Springs, Arizona
is the place to go

but she isn't ready, she'll never
be ready

the trucker can see that even from a distance
as he approaches her hitch-hiking the Ten in Walnut
he's seen lot lizards
looking better put-together than that

now that dog don't hunt! he mutters
into the CB radio to no-one

she looks like one of those days
that start perfectly fine
but then grind to a halt when you floor it

she's made up her face in the wrong mirror—
the classical mirror of introspection—
while in his mirror he sees nothing
not even what is behind him on the road

while ahead of him, the Day
has her thumb out as she practices
the rhumba along the center divider
and the trucker reaches his arm out the window
scooping her up by the waist
at eighty miles an hour
with both hands still on the wheel

what a vision she is as she tells him
all the lives she's lived
all the people she's been

the Druid who was dancing with her
showers mistletoe onto the trailer hauling trees

poor dumb trucker, he muses,
will be dancing on the head of a pin
talking nonsense
with his arms around a beautiful cadaver
once the stars' heavy shadows finish her off

and there we see him, his truck over the side,
trees and midnight scattered everywhere,
his tears wetting the match
as he laughs with the Druid over a cigarette,
wondering who she was and where she went

<<*c'est la guerre*>>,
the CB radio reminds them in English
—only the radio is off—
the tractor is in the woods, and Day diminished to
a scarlet fingernail of moon low in the west

NIAMA LESLIE WILLIAMS

Twenty Little Projects on the Way to Annihilation

white in a black sea
somehow make them go pop!
make them see me
black riding a bean chili wave.
my neighborhood tastes like salsa
runs through the fingers
like the snappy red dress on the *morena's* body
as she does that macarena thang
swinging dark hair
looking with black eyes that smell of a city built on a mudpile
a city that has forgotten the crack of paper sails
on ships that visited before colón
bearing black faces with wide noses and salt-free skin.
i was born in *la ciudad de los angeles*
into a family of l's: Lessie and Lewis
breeding Lewie Jr. and Leonard and me
Leslie become Niama
i wanted Africa and brown in my summons.

i am actually not black in a bean chili sea
when i go to work
at work i swim in low income brown
and a white that will blind you
two different places you see
the one of course sending an eviction notice
the white sea couldn't take my ancestors, my salsa breath,
my bringing of Howard U. to the Catholic Church.
onomatopoeia might work
if i had spoken the proper poetic terms,
confused them with my sharpened wit,
they never would have fired my Eliot-loving ass.
"you've got the small stuff down," she said
"it's the big stuff we've got to work on"
how did i know she meant comp theory
and how not to bring in the big names your first year?
the winning salvo of fired-dom was David Ulin Luis Alfaro and Michael Datcher
swallowing that whole she coughed up yale sputter
and sought to rid her office of a temple owl.

the "Boobie" this owl had been as a child
erred with naiveté
will focus on the students
create her downfall
exasperate her moody superiors.

salsa and chitlins i tell you!
a steady diet will turn the sea black!
la puta està loca
but the bargain basement desk asks
who is the *puta*
and why borrow my language?
brown hand on brown desk
and i am black
in a white sea
smelling of lard and pupusas and chilis
a machete close by
dripping red
the blood of a yale bandana.

TAMAR DIANA WILSON

Divorced Again

Divorce is a sunken ship.
It's me the waters boil over
salt-brine in nostrils and on
my tongue and skin.
I try to row the pelican to the shore:
It caws like a manacled crow
rustles its feathers like a twirp
jabbers its message
that I will drown
unless I learn to fly
over the Sierra Madres
como un pato en el invierno
perhaps with Sam or who knows who?
(The duck might. They mate for life).
Divorce is sudden freedom:
leaves you trembling, insecure
like a new born chick
as it staggers about
not knowing that someday
its head might be chopped off.
Will I remarry:
reinsert myself within a
dark sarcophagus
warmed to the bone by dampness
that inevitably arrives?
Or will I become a Buddhist nun
with my background as a Jewish convert
called Tam by a Catholic friend
now atheist—who has never read the
Old testament or my namesake's
unfortunate destiny
that of an abandoned woman who feeds children
by offering her body for a few scrambled coins?
Now I will be a whore.
I will not be a whore.
Just (have been/will be?) much married and much
touched by masculine domination
as that book by Pierre Bourdieu speaks of it,

clamours, shrieks of it
on the lower shadowed shelf
of my bookcase's philosophical bent.
I will be a pelican.

TERRY WOLVERTON

Hermano Grande

The phone line crackles like *lardon*
crisping in an iron skillet
as I call past midnight from the
south of France. Insomnia
is fertile soil; I'm rooted like
a sunflower in the sole phone
booth of this village where stone walls
have stood eight hundred years. Town square
deserted, café dark, bolted,
still the fountain burbles under
the watchful eye of *La Èglise.*
One dim light burns at the back of
la patisserie, air scented
with baked yeast and *chocolat.* Taste
of rust coils in my throat; I trace
cold glass with a fingertip. Your
voice rubs up and down my spine like
Smoky, gray cat who visits in
my white room called Heaven. I feel
uprooted here, *etrangère.* My
tongue wrestles unfamiliar
phrases, always pinned. Sometimes my
mute French gives way to broken
Spanish—another language I
can't speak—*si vous plait* succumbs to
por favor. Still I try to gain
command. "In Paris," I boast, "I
rode the Metro to someplace
I'd never been, didn't get lost, felt
all *chingona,"* warm to laughter
that bursts out of you, winds around
me like gold filament spun through
transatlantic wire. You've just come
home to the Pacific from New
York, paved island where your *amor*
has just moved, as if to stretch
the thread would draw you close.

Forgive me

now for wishing it would snap; the air
in heaven can be thin, lonely.
I should have seen her shadow in
your eyes those times we kissed. *¿Como
se dice* who I am to you
now? *Tarte aux cerises?* Every
lexicon is blank. No warning,
our connection pops; my ear fills
with the sizzle of absence.
Alone in my glass booth, I stare
into the dark. Stone walls mock me
with dumb fortitude; canopy
of constellations swirls above.
"Je me suis perdue," I plead, can't
read their map. I sigh, redial
thirty-four numbers. "Big Brother,"
you explain the interruption.
"Hermano Grande," I translate
in my addled tongue, make you laugh
again. *Fille de mer,* what is there
to say? Someday I'll let go this
barbed line that severs as it binds.
An answered prayer may yield only
loss of faith. But *que sera
sera*. The church bells whisper "Time
to dream." *Buenas noches. Bonne nuit.*

Mitsuye Yamada

Watching

Death loves me too much.
She walks about in stocking feet
and scatters flower petals down the aisles.
Tender organ music thunders in my ears.
Her gentle touch grates on my tongue
and the smell of urine seeps into the plants in the atrium.
Your friend Hirata-san rose out of Honokaa and said
I saw the women in the house washing your father's body.
Compassionate resentment flowed out of your eyes.
Dying slowly is effortless.
Your wafer thin skin absorbs the omelette
while dark spots begin to spread like toast.
You want to wear Hawaii-Five-O with your apple juice.
Shall we clip brittle curled toenails
over the manuscripts of art and science?
Our granddaughter does cartwheels as we giggle.
She didn't know her name was Redshoes.
I thought your tempered shadow would fade away suddenly
soft as nails driven into my hands.
We watched rapidly.
Itai! Itai!
The lift chair spreads itself and swallows you in
and you disappear into the morning sunset.
The island is only a frail of sound away
and peeks through the stained-glass window.

Liz Ahl was educated at Emerson College, at the University of Pittsburgh, and at the University of Nebraska-Lincoln. She teaches poetry, writing, literature and women's studies at Plymouth State College in New Hampshire. Her poems have appeared or are forthcoming in *The Women's Review of Books*, *The Formalist*, *Crab Orchard Review*, *Prairie Schooner*, and dozens of other literary journals.

"'Moon, Come Back, I Still Love You' is part of an evolving series about the Apollo Space Program. Since Simmerman was writing about the moon, turning the poem's premise around seemed like a fun way to explore my own project through experimental play."

Angela Ball's books of poetry include *Kneeling Between Parked Cars*, *Quartet*, *Possession*, and *The Museum of the Revolution: 58 Exhibits*. Her poetry has appeared in journals including *The New Yorker*, *The New Republic*, *Ploughshares*, *Poetry*, *Field*, *Mademoiselle*, *Partisan Review*, *Kenyon Review*, *Grand Street*, and *Boulevard*; as well as in *Best American Poetry 2001*. Awards for her work have included fellowships from the Mississippi Arts Commission and the National Endowment for the Arts. In spring of 1999, she served as Poet in Residence at the University of Richmond. She lives in Hattiesburg, Mississippi, where she teaches in the Center for Writers, University of Southern Mississippi, and serves as an associate editor for *Mississippi Review*.

"About the little projects that make up 'Not About Lummoxes': Writing the poem resembled flying a kite—I found myself running back and forth to catch the currents I needed. The projects were a given, like the air, and like the air they could be negotiated in endless ways. It was nice to forget the ground and concentrate on the bright shape that I was trying to keep airborne."

Pat Barber: "I own a business and get up at 5:00 a.m. to write most days, plus stealing whatever time I can find. Have been part of a writing group for past two years that meets at Salem College's Center for Women Writers and just started sending stuff off a year ago. Have placed in several contests and have two poems in this year's *Award-Winning Poems* published by the NC Poetry Society. Have won short story and poetry prizes and have been Writer in Residence at the Weymouth Center for Arts and Humanities. Just completed my first novel, *Chasing the Moon* which I have just begun to try to place with an agent."

Solomon Bass: "I was born in Chicago, IL, on June 14th, 1994. I go to Crow Island School. I have one older brother and one younger sister. I tried to write when I was four, but I always did my 'S' backwards. I've been making things up for five years. I like ballet. I'm interested in China.

"When I started writing this poem it was hard, and after a while I got bored, but when the poem was done, it sounded funny."

Grace Bauer has published a full length collection of poems, *The Women at the Well* (Portals Press) and three chapbooks, the most recent of which is *Field Guide to the Ineffable: Poems on Marcel Duchamp*. Her poems and stories have appeared in numerous journals, including *American Literary Review, Colorado Review, Georgia Review, Poetry*, and others.

"The 'caprice' aspect of the 'The Twenty Little Poetry Projects' is what I most enjoyed. It led me to some interesting leaps in narrative, while still allowing a story to unfold in the poem. When first experimenting with a form I haven't tried before, I often find myself writing a poem that comments—or speaks to—the form itself, and so here, my 'Lunacy' speaks to Jim Simmerman's 'Moon Go Away . . .' And Jim gave me the line about 'cesspools and Circle K.'"

Robin Becker's fifth collection of poems, *The Horse Fair*, was published in 2000 by the University of Pittsburgh Press. That year, she won the George W. Atherton Award for Excellence in Teaching, a university-wide prize, from the Pennsylvania State University where she is Professor of English and Women's Studies.

"In writing 'Bi-Polar Pets,' I abandoned my usual lyrical and narrative impulses. Instead, I followed the trail of instructions (like a path of bread crumbs or a series of clues) and thereby both discovered and uncovered a set of characters and a story-line I would otherwise have missed."

Wendy Bishop teaches writing at Florida State University. The author of *Thirteen Ways of Looking for a Poem: A Guide to Writing Poetry*, her five chapbooks, include *Mid-Passage* and *My 47 Lives*.

"Before using writing exercises in class, I try them myself. In 1981, I taught at Northern Arizona University with Jim Simmerman, so I turned to his 'The Twenty Little Poetry Projects' in *The Practice of Poetry* and took it for this test drive. I like the way it allowed me to fuse elements of a new-to-me Florida landscape to a sharp little love lament. Seeing the results, I was ready to share the poem and exercise with others."

Hannah Bleier: "I am an infinitesimal speck in an limitless universe, a teacher and slightly-published writer-speck living in Los Angeles with mourning doves, dogs of all sizes, wild parrots, and all kinds of people eating, meditating, praying, talking, doing laundry, kissing, fighting, driving, walking alone, and thinking various things they don't say.

"I found the exercise relaxing, because I could suspend the pressure I feel to do something original when confronted with a blank page, and simply do as I was told. I got very involved in it, missed dinner, and went to bed far too late."

Linda Bosson is an editor at the wire service of *The New York Times*. Her poetry has appeared in *Green Mountains Review, Hawaii Pacific Review, Yankee, Writer's Digest, Prairie Winds,* and other publications.

Gayle Brandeis is the author of *Fruitflesh: Seeds of Inspiration for Women Who Write* (Harper San Francisco). Her novel *The Book of Dead Birds* won the 2002 Bellwether Prize in Support of a

Literature of Social Change, and was published by HarperCollins in 2003. She lives in River-side, CA, with her husband and two children.

"Poetry projects like this often lead to more surprise, more playfulness and immediacy with language, than the poems that spill from me organically. What a fun challenge this was, a constant astonishment."

Susan Buis recently moved to Los Angeles from the Canadian prairies, where she had a career as an artist, curator, and art gallery administrator. She came to writing through the production of artist books with text and images. She is the mother of two and is currently studying Art History and English at Cal State Long Beach. The poem "Domestic Bliss" was written as a class assignment.

Pamela Burke is a writer, fabric artist, and social psychologist in Middletown, NJ.

She writes, "After several practice excursions using this form on more mundane topics, I found myself drawn to September 11, a subject I had been unwilling to write about for months. 'The Twenty Little Poetry Projects' prodded me to keep going— 'Oh, just try one more line, go ahead . . .'—when I wanted to crawl into a ball and cry. Maybe only a form that embraces the absurd could help me make sense of my experience of this devastating event."

Patricia Carlin's work has appeared in many journals. *Original Green*, a collection of her poetry, was published by Marsh Hawk Press in spring 2003. She co-edits the poetry journal *Barrow Street,* and she teaches literature and poetry writing at New School University.

"I go back to 'The Twenty Little Poetry Projects' periodically, and follow the recipe as whim dictates. Sometimes (as for the poem in this anthology) I revise drastically; other times the poem almost writes itself. I find the exercise really useful for students, too. Some things this exercise have done for me and for my students: shake up writers who are stuck in narrative, or logical thinking, or autobiography, or unvarying diction, or an overly insistent 'self' (which self?), or an excess of seriousness, or . . . or . . . or. . . ."

Marie Cartier has performed poetry, monologues and body based art extensively around the West Coast. She is the author and performer of two full length one woman shows—*Ballistic Femme* and *Blessed Virgin*, both premiered in Los Angeles, (*Ballistic Femme* at Highways Performance Space and *Blessed Virgin* at LATC). She is the author of the poetry book, *I Am Your Daughter, Not Your Lover*, published by Clothespin Fever Press, and five published plays through Dialogus Press. Currently she teaches Women's Studies at Cal State Northridge, screenwriting at UC Irvine, and is a dual degree student at Claremont Graduate University, working on her Ph.D. in Religion, specializing in Religion and Art as well as Women and Religion, and her MFA in Art.

"I loved writing the poetry exercise . . . it opens that wonderful space where you have freedom with control . . . and that is how to take a 'big dic' trip!"

Helen Marie Casey's poetry has been published in several literary journals, including *The Larcom Review, The Laurel Review, Calyx, America, The Connecticut Review, The Worcester Review, Northeast Corridor,* and *Windhover.* Her columns appear Sundays in the *MetroWest Daily News.*

"Responding to suggestions like those from 'The Twenty Little Poetry Projects' invited the following in my poem: the elimination of the poetry censor; the freeing of the creative imagination; and the welcoming in of serendipity in the creative process. It was great fun to follow instructions like this one: 'Make a declarative assertion that sounds convincing but that finally makes no sense.'"

George Chacon is a first generation Costa Rican-American and Los Angeles native, residing in San Francisco. George has read at many venues and is a repeat participant in The National Poetry Foundation's Poetry in Motion program, honoring National Poetry Month. His work can be seen at the online journal of poetry, *The Kenwood Review.*

Of "You feel empty as fire" he writes: "I often struggle with ghosts . . . their reasons and lack of rationale. I give voice to their voices, and dedicate this poem to the ghost of my highly imaginative and supportive grandmother, Elba Alvarado, and the artist, Eva Hesse; these 'projects' are like the windows of their worlds."

Danielle Cohn is a freelance writer, editor and translator. She has written for theme parks and museums, and has been published in *Poetry* magazine and *Free 2 Wheel*, a motorcycle enthusiast magazine.

"I first attempted to write this poem with a specific subject in mind, but felt some of the lines sounded too forced. In following the line prompts a second time, without a specific subject in mind, I deepened my understanding of how the subject and form interact, and was able to revise the first poem."

Rita D. Costello received her BFA from Bowling Green State University, her MFA from Wichita State University, and is finishing her Ph.D. at the University of Louisiana in Lafayette where she also teaches. She has published work in *Glimmer Train, ACM, Baltimore Review, New Delta Review, Chattahoochee Review, Fireweed,* and elsewhere. She is the co-editor of the anthology *Bend Don't Shatter: Poets on the Beginning of Desire*, from Soft Skull Press. Her work has been nominated for the Pushcart Prize.

She says of "empty tanks by firelight": "Although I am not a formalist in any sense, I am very conscious of creating patterns and forms in each poem I write. 'The Twenty Little Poetry Projects' appealed to that sense of internally creating forms; I carried the rules around with me for weeks, trying out a poem whenever I had the chance."

Karin Cotterman is a native Californian who wrote "The wayward possum of life" while living in the Midwest. She writes, "We lived in an apartment directly off what used to be part of Route 66. The semis were so loud we didn't open the windows. I love this exercise . . . everything that was on my mind made its way into the poem . . . my mother speaking Swedish, the culture shock of moving to the Midwest from San Francisco, the ridiculously white manger scenes popular at Christmas time . . . even a little nod to WCW at the end." Her work has been published in *Bayou, Icarus, Coracle, Fourteen Hills*, and other journals. Her e-mail address is karin_cotterman@yahoo.com.

Catherine Daly is the author of two books of poetry, *Locket* (Tupelo Press: 2004), and the trilogy *DaDaDa* (Salt Publishing: 2003). She plays with constraints frequently.

"While these constraints weren't particularly generative or informative for me, I put subject matter I use frequently 'through the paces.' For example, it is useful to force writers unaware of metaphor to look it up, but being challenged to include a metaphor in my first line didn't change my habits.

"In renga, there are so many constraints that while the individual responses keep a personal quality, they assemble around approaches. Like those, this collection of constraint-based poems reveals my habits or 'stamp' to me, and those of the other contributors as well—what a valuable meta-anthology!"

Jenny Davidson: "Utilizing 'The Twenty Little Poetry Projects' expelled me from familiar rhythms of language. The process forced exploration, humor, completion amidst resistance. These projects possessed my pen almost nonsensically and enabled me to unearth subjects and word connections that I could not touch consciously; the experience of these projects was like entering into a color as opposed to writing the word yellow.

I was born and raised in Dallas, Texas (though there is more Brooklyn than Dallas in me, thanks to my parents). I presently live in Los Angeles with my cat Claude. This poem is my first published work."

John Davis lives on Bainbridge Island, Washington. A high school teacher, he plays in the blues-rock-reggae band Never Been To Utah. His poetry appears in several journals including *Beloit Poetry Journal, The Laurel Review, Passages North* and *Poetry Northwest*. He formerly edited *The Duckabush Journal*.

"'The Twenty Little Poetry Projects' form allows writers to write a poem without thinking about a poem. The twists and turns help writers understanding how pliable a poem can be."

Jessica de Koninck is an attorney and public policy analyst. Her poems appear in *The Jewish Women's Literary Annual, Exit 13, Higginsville Reader, Ruah* and elsewhere.

"Much of my poetry has a surrealistic quality. So, the exercise was not inconsistent with how I write, but more formally structured, like writing a sonnet, with the focus on content rather than rhyme and meter. I carried the list everywhere while working on the first draft over many days. Normally, I write a first draft in one or two sittings. Once I had incorporated the twenty requirements I revised primarily for narrative consistency and to highlight sound.

Yvonne M. Estrada has been a member of the Women's Poetry Project in Los Angeles for seven years. She contributed work to *(en)closures*, and the compilation of poem series *Catena*, both publications of the WPP.

"'The Twenty Little Poetry Projects' offers structure and freedom to break out of the structure. It brings on the brainstorm and the challenge. It gets the poem done."

Mary Florio has taught English for over twenty years. Her work has been published in several magazines, including *The Paterson Literary Review, Lips, The Ever Dancing Muse*, the *English Journal*, the *New Jersey English Journal, Wings*, and *Sensations Magazine*. She has won several prizes for her poetry, including second place in the 1997 Allen Ginsberg poetry competition. In addition, she is one of the founding members of HillPoets and a member of No Retreat, a women's writing collective.

"Even though most of my work is free verse, I love working in form. Some say that even my 'free-est' of free verse poems contain some kind of inherent structure. I enjoyed the challenge of this exercise, the container that contains one leap after another, the ability to free fall into the surreal while revealing the mysterious story of the poem. The day I received the information about the contest, I had had a conversation/debate with a friend about the merits of asparagus. I teach high school English and, yes, we were studying *Hamlet*. How would Hamlet have felt about asparagus, if he could have gotten his hands on some? Thus, the poem."

Cherryl Floyd-Miller has held fellowships in Idyllwild (2003), Caldera (2002), Cave Canem (1998-2000), the Vermont Studio Center (1997), and the Indiana Arts Commission (1994-95). Her work has appeared or is forthcoming in *North Carolina Literary Review, storySouth, Crab Orchard Review, Beyond the Frontier*, and *Keeping the Faith*. Her first collection of poems, *Utterance: a Museology of Kin*, was a semifinalist for the 2001 Kathryn A. Morton Prize in Poetry. She lives in Atlanta, where she is the 2004 Fulton County Arts Council DIALOG Fellow. A second collection of poems, *Chops*, is scheduled for release July 2004 by Nexus Press.

"I wrote 'bountiful' after a Thanksgiving visit here in Atlanta from my family. I moderate an online poetry group called MonkeyBREAD, and our current writing exercise was the 'The Twenty Little Poetry Projects' by Jim Simmerman. When my family left me to return to North Carolina, I tried to write a thank you for them and couldn't. All that would come to me were bright images (recent and ancient) of all these people I'd known for so many years. Frustrated, I sat down to work on the MonkeyBREAD writing exercise, and 'bountiful' was born."

Kate Gale lives in Los Angeles and teaches at Loyola Marymount University. She is the author of four books of poetry, a novel, a children's book and the editor of three anthologies.

"This is the second time Terry has invited me into the process of writing a poem in a form that I was not used to. The first time was a prose poetry project. In both cases, I was jolted out of my comfort zone of writing poetry in a manner and form that I had fallen into and asked to try another method and step into being another poet. In both cases, I have grown as a poet and been surprised by the energy and quality of the work that emerged."

Richard Garcia is the author of *Rancho Notorious*, BOA Editions. His poems have recently appeared in the web publications *Perihelion, The Blue Moon Review, The Cortland Review,* and in the print journals *Sentence* and *Pool*. His website is www.richardgarcia.info

"Using 'The Twenty Little Poetry Projects' is not too different from how I usually hope to write a poem. I gave the projects to my students. As far as I know, five of my students were accepted in the anthology. 'The Twenty Little Poetry Projects' provides platforms to jump off of, a good distraction from the obsessive self-preoccupation of writing a poem, narrative and tonal shifts and juxtapositions, and a concentration on line by line improvisation. I am now encouraging my students to make and share their own twenty projects. I feel a writing exercise, no matter how good the poem that comes out of it, is incomplete unless the student learns how to recreate that place for themselves."

Ryn Gargulinski is a poet, writer and artist who writes an illustrated column for *12gauge.com*. Her work, which ranges from haiku to a Master's thesis on the Folklore of NYC Subway Workers, can be found in numerous publications, in her three illustrated chapbooks, other online stores at cafeshops.com/rynindustries, and on her website at ryngargulinski.com. She holds an MA and a BFA from Brooklyn College.

"This project was particularly amusing, especially the absurdity of it all. I began by wondering what my favorite composer's music would taste like—it ended up being one of my favorite fruits! From there, I just followed directions and it all fell into place (ironically, harmoniously)."

Pamela Garvey has published poetry in such journals as *Sonora Review, South Carolina Review, Sou'wester, Pleiades, Yemassee,* and *The Santa Barbara Review*. She has an MFA in creative writing from Virginia Commonwealth University and MA in English from the University of Missouri-Columbia. She is an English professor at St. Louis Community College-Meramec.

"Regarding 'The Twenty Little Poetry Projects,' I found this exercise both challenging and great fun. I often begin poems with some kind of exercise, whether it's one I've invented or something as traditional as a sonnet, and this exercise was exciting to me because it combined so many different aspects of poetry in one project. What is so pleasurable and freeing about such exercises is that I surprise myself. In this poem, I came up with the opening metaphor and knew only that I was writing about lovers from the male's perspective. From there, I had to find out who this character was and what he felt. The twenty projects equipped me with tools to find that out. Without those tools, I wouldn't have made the turns I did, and ultimately those turns make the poem successful."

William Greenway's seventh collection, *Ascending Order*, is forthcoming from the University of Akron Press Poetry Series, which also published *I Have My Own Song For It: Modern Poems of Ohio* (2002), which he co-edited. He has a new collection, *Fishing at the End of the World*, forthcoming from Word Press. His publications include *Poetry, American Poetry Review, Poetry Northwest, Southern Review, Shenandoah,* and *Prairie Schooner*. He's won numerous awards, most recently the 2001 Ohioana Poetry Award, and is professor of English at Youngstown State University.

"I use this exercise in my poetry writing class to pry students out of their linear and logical thinking. We discuss Robert Bly's term 'leaping poetry,' and how illogic, or disjunction, often reveals unsuspected affinities between ideas, affinities that are given cohesion by their own personalities. Almost anything they write, I tell them, will form a pattern they were not aware existed in their own subconscious, and that poets are just people with a love of language who've learned to listen to themselves, to the part of themselves that most people only encounter in their dreams. I knew that if I did the exercise with them, it would work for me, too, because William Stafford has taught me that 'a writer is not so much someone who has something to say as he is someone who has found a process that will bring about new things that he would not have thought of if he hadn't started to say them.' In other words, we don't get inspired and then write; we get inspired *as* we write. And Jim Simmerman has provided us with a model for an excellent kind of process. (Incidentally, the suicide Easter egg is the last one you dye, and so dip in *all* the colors. The Simmerman exercise often produces what I think of as quilt, collage, or batik effects.)"

John Grey: Australian born poet, playwright, musician. Winner of the 1998 Rhysling Award for Speculative Poetry and much published in many journals including *South Carolina Review, Poet Lore*, and *Cape Rock*.

"The exercise itself I found stimulating. Having a skeleton, as it were, gave me much more room in my imagination for the flesh I chose to wrap around it. Sometimes restrictions can free you."

Dina Hardy, winner of the 2003 *Smartish Pace* Erskine J. Poetry Prize, was also a finalist for the 2004 *Poets & Writers'* California Voices Contest.

"While writing 'Stitching Up the Past,' I kept a sheet of paper covering the twenty instructions and I would slide the paper down to expose one direction at a time. This process forced me to build the poem line by line. It also created an element of surprise that required me to abandon any preconceived notions of what I thought this poem would be about when I started writing it."

Pamela Harrelson: "I received my MFA from Antioch University and teach English at a community college in Northern California. My work has been published in *4ᵗʰ Street, Penumbra, Crux, The San Francisco Chronicle*, and several on-line magazines. I consider myself an essayist who writes poetry as a diversionary tactic against taking myself too seriously. Playing with Jim Simmerman's strategy was just the poetic adventure I delight in. The prompts took me beneath the clutter of thought process, closer to the synapses in my belly, fingertips, and knees. This poem comes from my cellular memory, raw and reactionary."

Stephanie Hemphill has recently published work in *California Quarterly* and *Lungfull! Magazine*, and her series of poems, *Story of a Girl in Mirrored Room*, appeared in Fall 2003 as a part of a collection called *Catena*. Stephanie's first novel in poems, *Things Left Unsaid*, is forthcoming from Hyperion in March 2005.

"'The Twenty Little Poetry Projects' is a fabulous exercise because it forces me to abandon my intentions to those of the poem. I didn't know what 'Prayer' was about until I had written it. I love the surprise and the surrender this exercise encourages."

Michael Hoerman lives with his wife and daughter in Cambridge, Mass. His poetry has recently appeared in the *Arkansas Literary Forum, Potomac Review, Chiron Review*, and several anthologies. His first chapbook, *Bad Rotten*, was recently published by Pudding House. Website: www.badrotton.com.

"The poem included in this anthology, 'Pentecost,' is the result of 'The Twenty Little Poetry Projects,' a bottle of cheap red wine, an old girlfriend living across town, too many holier-than-thou Cambridge poetry events and a host of other factors that can't be gotten into in polite company."

Noah Hoffenberg is a poet living in Vermont. He is the author *of The Man with Two Heads*, and the editor of *The Brink: An Anthology of Postmodern Poetry, 1965 to the present*, both published by Yeti Press.

"The poetry projects came to me via Richard 'The True Poet' Garcia. The projects opened up a wild and wooly world of intuition and synchronicity for me. I have since mapped some of my favorite poems as poetry projects, and written more of this type of poetry. Whoever said there was no magic formula to writing good poetry was dead wrong."

Abha Iyengar is an Indian writer who writes in all genres, but prefers to write creative nonfiction and poetry. Publications include an article on, "Population" for the book *Science, Technology and Development* (Wiley Eastern: 1991) a prize winning haiku in *Life Positive*, and poems in *Femina*. She has received a Breakaway Books Contest Honorable Mention and publication. She is a Kota Press Poetry Anthology Contest Winner. Her articles/essays/poems have appeared in *Writer's Hood, Shy Librarian, Artemis, Insolent Rudder, It's About Time Writers, Raven Chronicles, Gowanus Books, Tattoo Highway, 3 Tryst, M.A.G., Surface Online, Door Knobs*, and *Body Paint*, among others. E-mail: abha_iyengar@hotmail.com, abhaiyengar @rediffmail.com

Robin Jacobson: "Publisher of True North Press (www.truenorthpress.com), I teach through California Poets in the Schools and Poets & Writers, and have been published and honored by some of the usual suspects (to see more of my poems, visit www.webdelsol.com/mudlark or www.unf.edu/mudlark). When I start with an idea or emotional urgency, I often labor over a poem only to see it die in childbirth, but I wrote 'The Opposite of Seeds' in record time, a clear message about letting go of trying. Also, 'composting'—recycling strong images from flawed poems—helps me see those earlier pieces not as failures but as part of a continuity in my writing life."

Rhoda Janzen held the California Poet Laureate Award in '94 and '97. Some of the journals in which she has appeared recently include *The Yale Review, The Gettysburg Review, Poetry Midwest, Borderlands, The Malahat Review, The Ledge*, and *American Literary Review*. In 2001 she appeared in the PBS television series *Closer To Truth*. Her academic work focuses on constructions of gender and deceit—she's interested in America's history of treating women and girls as somehow more dishonest than men and boys. Currently she teaches American Literature and Creative Writing at Hope College in Holland, Michigan.

"This sonnet was inspired by a friend who told me she had come across a weird Bible verse, Jeremiah 17:9: 'The heart is deceitful beyond all cure.' Because my dissertation looked at constructions of gender and deceit in American culture, I am especially intrigued by the idea of self-deception, that process that so many women undergo in order to accommodate the larger culture's expectations for gendered behavior. For women, it's often easier to deny that they manipulate others through their sexuality than it is to face the knowledge that they live in a culture that offers them no alternative to this role.

"So I wanted to create a self-deceiving female speaker. I figured that the best way to reveal her level of denial and lack of self-awareness would be to project her sensibility onto a series of nonhuman objects. I imagined her in bed very early one morning, and the stuff around her— her cat, her blanket, her belly-button ring—begin to speak with each other. Together they reveal the limitations of her world."

Allison Joseph is the author of five collections, including *In Every Seam* (University of Pittsburgh Press: 1997) and *Imitation of Life* (Carnegie-Mellon University Press: 2003). She lives, teaches, and edits in Carbondale, Illinois, where's she's part of the creative writing faculty at Southern Illinois University.

Gina Larkin: "I have retired from teaching high school and currently am Editor of the *Edison Literary Review*. I have had sixty poems published. When a friend said I should try this exercise, I said 'I can't do this.' But I tried anyway, the challenge I guess, and was really surprised at the results. I did not think that I could let myself write in what seemed so many unconnected tangents or that it would take me to that stoop in Brooklyn so long ago. It's quite wonderful when the poem moves to where IT wants to go."

Michael Lassell is the author of three books of poems, including the Lambda Literary Award-winning *Decade Dance* (Alyson) and, most recently *A Flame for the Touch That Matters* (Painted Leaf Press.) He has also edited several volumes of poetry, including (with Elena Georgiou) *The World in Us: Lesbian and Gay Poetry of the Next Wave* (St. Martin's Press).

"'The Twenty Little Poetry Projects' was a revelation to me. Not only did it get me to writing, but it liberated my vocabulary and imagery, and loosened me up in every way. It also gave me a structure for a poem that starts with the fact that it was written on the day that George Harrison died. It reminded me that it is probably better if a poem does not begin with the first-person singular pronoun. And it pushed the content of the poem beyond my own feelings to a broader, more global (and even ultimately more positive) point of view."

Betty Lies is a poet in the schools for the New Jersey State Council on the Arts and the Geraldine R. Dodge Foundation. She has published poems in numerous journals, and she is the author of four books, the most recent of which is *Earth's Daughters: Stories of Women in Classical Mythology* (Fulcrum.) She has received grants for poetry from NJSCA and the Vermont Studio Center, and won the Governor's Award in Arts Education, 2000.

"Writing to 'The Twenty Little Poetry Projects' exercise liberated me to say things I wouldn't have otherwise, to take risks and to make imaginative leaps."

Diane Lockward's collection, *Eve's Red Dress*, was published by Wind Publications in 2003. Her poems have appeared in *Spoon River, North American Review, Prairie Schooner, The Beloit Poetry Journal,* and elsewhere. Her work has been nominated for three Pushcart Prizes, featured twice on Poetry Daily, and read by Garrison Keillor on NPR's *The Writer's Almanac.*

Of *"Felis Rufus,"* Diane says, "among my kids' old school papers, I found a metaphor my son had written in second grade: 'I am wild as a bobcat.' Years later I was struck by the metaphor's sweetness and strangeness. I started my poem with that metaphor and then let it take over. An internet search provided my title and some specific details about the bobcat. I eliminated much of the original draft, did some rearranging, and formatted to simulate the bobcat's pacing as well as his jagged ledge. The wackiness of the prompt led me through unfamiliar territory, forcing me to proceed in a non-linear fashion."

Joel T. Long's book *Winged Insects* won the White Pine Press Poetry Prize and was published in 1999. His poems have appeared in *Prairie Schooner, Mid-American Review, Sonora Review,* and *Willow Springs,* among others. His poems have also appeared in the anthologies *American Poetry: the Next Generation* and *Essential Love.* He teaches creative writing in West Jordan, Utah, where he founded the Lake Effect Writers Conference in 1996.

"I have used 'The Twenty Little Poetry Projects' in my classes to loosen the control that students have over their poems and open up the process to surprise and discovery generated by allowing the poem to be informed by the music of language. This exercise helps because each new task forces the writer into something he didn't expect. As Miles Davis once said to a young sax player, 'You already said that. Play something new.'"

Janet McCann: "Journals publishing my poems include *Kansas Quarterly, Parnassus, Nimrod, Sou'wester, New York Quarterly, Tendril, PoetryAustralia,* and *McCall's.* Have won three chapbook contests, sponsored by Pudding Publications, Chimera Connections, and Franciscan University Press. A 1989 NEA Creative Writing Fellowship winner, I have taught at Texas A&M University since 1969, am currently coordinator of creative writing here. Have co-edited two anthologies, *Odd Angles of Heaven* (1994) and *Place of Passage* (Story Line: 2000). Most recent poetry book: *Looking for Buddha in the Barbed Wire Garden* (Avisson: 1996). Most recent book: *In a Field of Words*, textbook, co-authored with Sybil Estess (Prentice Hall: 2002)."

Frances Ruhlen McConnel: "Besides *Mudlark,* I've published poetry in the Web journals *Salt River Review, 2 River Review,* and *Stirring Mag* as well as in such regular journals as *Soho, International Poetry Review, The Seattle Review, The Massachusetts Review,* and *Iowa Review.* Pygmalion Press published my book of poems, *Gathering Light.* I also edited for them an anthology of West

Coast Women Poets, *One Step Closer*. I also write and publish essays and fiction and am presently writing an eccentric family memoir, parts of which have appeared in the Web journal *Sprawlopolis*. This winter a poem of mine won the Oneiros Press Broadside Contest and another poem came in fourth in the LA Art Project contest. I am on the verge of leaving my teaching position at the University of California at Riverside to write full time.

"'We Dream of Heroes' was published in 2001 by the Web journal *Mudlark: www.unf.edu/mudlark*. It began in a workshop where I teach at the University of California in Riverside. I had given them the Simmerman exercise and was writing along with them. I'd been working on poems about my father, who worked on the Manhattan Project and died of cancer, probably as a result of his work. I got started by running over the projects in my head: a place, lots of sensual detail, a language other than English—bird language, words I'd never seen in a poem—'slow as smoke from shit'—a phrase that delighted me as a child as I had never heard my mother use that word before. In fact, the idea of the forbidden kept popping up at me from this assignment. Thinking also of my father, I focused on one of the most sensual experiences from our years in Oak Ridge, Tennessee: camping on the banks of Lake Wattsbar."

"My name is **Julia McGarey**. I graduated from Texas A&M University with a degree in English, and I plan to pursue an MFA in creative writing. I have always had good results with poetry exercises, so I enjoyed working with 'The Twenty Little Poetry Projects' exercise. I find that having specific guidelines to follow helps me make better use of my words. When you are given a set of guidelines, you have to be innovative to make the poem your own."

Phil Meyer's poetry has appeared in the *Berkeley Poetry Review, POZ Magazine, Modern Words, Art and Understanding,* and *Blood Whispers, Volume 2.* In addition to being a writer, Phil is an opera singer, clinical social worker and psychotherapist in private practice. He lives in Los Angeles with his partner, Kenneth Robins, and their children Lily and Ruben.

"Conforming to the structure of 'The Twenty Little Poetry Projects' freed me to write the 'dirtiest' poem I have ever put on paper."

Peggy Miller leads poetry workshops for senior citizens and is an Associate Editor for *The Comstock Review*. She holds an MFA from American University where she studied under Henry Taylor. She is author of two chapbooks, *Martha Contemplates the Universe* (Frith Press), and one in Pudding House's Greatest Hits series. Her poems have appeared in many journals. She lives in The Villages, FL, with her husband Phil Wolfson, and is the mother of three grown children.

"Was this different from the way I usually write a poem? It sure was! I've owned Behn & Twitchell for years and I remember the first time I read Jim Simmerman's 'The Twenty Little Poetry Projects.' I thought, this is exactly what gives poetry a bad name. (A poem must communicate, must be grammatical!) Then last May I attended a poetry workshop with Tom Ward in Syracuse, NY. It was an intense workshop about metaphor during which we wrote a poem using Simmerman's exercise. And that day I got it! You didn't just make a random sequence of meaningless statements. You began with a story to tell, and you told it in cooperation with Simmerman. The strangeness of the questions gave the writing a wondrous quirkiness, a poetic sense we all dream about harnessing. With very little change from that fist draft, I wrote 'Education.' A word about its 'left-turn' ending–I was grasping for a way out. We sat in a dull green room; in the corner stood a YMCA (not Salvation Army) flag, its gold tassel edging coming loose. I simply worked that observation into the image."

Jeff Mock is the author of a chapbook, *Evening Travelers* (Volans Press: 1994), and a guidebook for beginning writers, *You Can Write Poetry* (Writer's Digest Books: 1998). His poems appear in *The Atlantic Monthly, Crazyhorse, The Georgia Review, The Iowa Review, New England Review, The North American Review, Poetry Northwest, Quarterly West, The Sewanee Review, Shenandoah, The Southern Review,* and elsewhere. He teaches at Southern Connecticut State University, where he regularly uses "The Twenty Little Poetry Projects" in his poetry-writing courses.

"Working with Jim Simmerman's 'The Twenty Little Poetry Projects' was an exhilarating exercise in controlling chaos. It freed me from my usual logical thought process, allowing me to go nuts on the page, while the demands of creating a coherent whole forced me to maintain a focus, no matter how absurd the language, images, and situation became. The first line—the first project, the metaphor—arrived unexpectedly and ended up generating the whole poem. The tension inherent in the image of John Wayne in a tutu fixed the subject matter and tone, and I tried just to keep up as the projects essentially wrote the poem. The exercise presented me with the poem, a gift."

Laura Moe: "I hold a MFA in creative nonfiction from Goucher College, and teach writing and literature part-time at Ohio University-Zanesville, and full-time at Maysville Middle School. I have published poetry and prose in several journals, including *Women's Words, Pudding House, Ohio Teachers Write, The Cleveland Plain Dealer, Riverwind, Brevity* and *5 AM.* My YA novel, *Parallel Lines,* (under the pen name Coyote Gordon) has gotten good reviews and is used in several school at-risk programs.

"I love doing this exercise. It is an excellent way to pull yourself out of writer's block as it forces you to focus line by line and concentrate on form, yet also a generate a flow. In my original drafts each time I do the exercise, I write each line by following the format. Once I have the lines down, I move them around for the best surge of the poem. I often torture my Creative Writing students with it, and they create amazing poems that get them out of their comfort zones. I find middle school students are more responsive than college kids at trying something out of the box.

"This particular poem was inspired by my father's World War II experience. He was a teenager living in Honolulu during Pearl Harbor. Like most of his generation, the war dominated his life. He still shrinks from the sound of fireworks on Fourth of July, and I wonder if he is recalling the noise of war."

Leslie Monsour's work has appeared in *POETRY Magazine, The Formalist, The Dark Horse, The Edge City Review, The Plum Review, Hellas, The Lyric, Fourteen Hills,* and the online journal, *Able Muse.* She has published three collections of poetry: *Earth's Beauty, Desire, & Loss* (Robert L.

Barth: 1998); *Indelibility* (Aralia Press: 1999); *Travel Plans* (Robert L. Barth: 2001). Her work was nominated by Anthony Hecht for the 2001 Pushcart Prize.

"This exercise gave me the opportunity to free-associate, abandon logic, and revel in nonsequiturs. It was entertaining and limbering. I feel as though I've written a John Ashbery poem."

Jim Natal's first full-length collection, *In the Bee Trees* (Archer Books: 2000), was a finalist for the 2001 Pen Center West and Publisher's Marketing Association Ben Franklin Awards. A second collection, *Talking Back to the Rocks*, will be published by Archer Books in 2003. His poetry recently has appeared or is forthcoming in *Pool, The Paterson Literary Review, The Yalobusha Review, Solo, Clay Palm Review, Rattle,* and *Cafe Review*. Natal was one of the winners of the 2003 Poetry in the Windows contest sponsored by the Arroyo Arts Collective. Natal currently teaches the Plein Air poetry workshop in Joshua Tree National Park in conjunction with the Desert Institute, and is the curator and co-host of the monthly Poem.X series in Santa Monica. He founded Conflu:X Press in 2004.

"The exercise was a map to an ongoing series of poems, taken out of context of time and place. They incorporate less linear narrative construction, riskier leaps, and foreign words and phrases, while still maintaining lyric sensibility. It added new tools to my poetry tool belt and helped to free up my writing."

Molly Nelson: "I am a senior at Minnesota State University, Mankato, majoring in English with a Sociology minor. I loved working with 'The Twenty Little Poetry Projects.' It is a great way to write a poem with a very flexible set of guidelines, allowing one to get outrageously creative. I had no inspiration for the poem. It just sort of popped into my head and sounded dirty and interesting to me."

Eve Nicholas is a freelance writer, currently living with her husband in Austin, TX. Her work has appeared in *The Spoon River Poetry Review, The Midwest Quarterly* and *Borderlands: Texas Poetry Review*, and is forthcoming in an anthology by Putnum Publishing Group. About "Playground," Eve writes: "I rarely attempt poetry exercises because I usually write out of a much more organic place: I find an intriguing image and build the poem from there. This exercise took me further out of my 'comfort zone' by not allowing me to craft the poem as I usually do. The result is a poem written by my hand, but based on someone else's process and rules."

Sharose Niedelman is a Native Californian/Angeleno-Valley Girl, emerging poetess, creative and technical writer/researcher, mixed-media artist, and art educator with a unique flair for cartoons, collage, paint, digital media, and teaching children. Sharose's current works-in-progress span creating poetry-art videos, new media installation/performance, healing mandala art, and developing creativity tools, toys, games, media and paper products. Her words range from the whimsical to contemplative, celebrating and questioning love, and observant writings about nature and humanity with rare insight, sensuality, and wit. *Recently,* her first chapbook, is composed of poetry dating from 1997 to 2001. Be certain to look out for Sharose's stylings of fiction, lyrical song, and children's stories.

"This process challenged me to open up to new formats and combinations of ideas that I had previously not explored. It made me take a look at how I might use grammar to my advantage. I especially enjoyed integrating slang and specifically a line of a foreign language. I randomly wrote one liners and had them transcribed by a friend and looked at the rhythm to see how the words flowed within the poem, whether or not it made all that much sense in its meaning. These lines turned out to give an added nonsensical flavor and fresh aliveness in my creative process, and a hidden dimension that made it all the more fun to do! I treated each project independent of the other with great focus, yet wanted the concept to somehow thread and make some type of sense in coming full circle from beginning to end. The original metaphor giving birth to this poem was from a personal archived image in my head that opened up with an elaboration on the senses. What I imagined in doing these individual experiments was my hand actually going into a different pocket and pulling a new toy out to play with, like Play-doh."

Jamie O'Halloran was born on Long Island, raised there, and in New Orleans and Seattle. She is the author of the chapbook *Sweet to the Grit* and her poems have appeared in *Prairie Schooner, Solo, The Cream City Review* and other magazines. She lives in Los Angeles where she teaches in a public middle school.

"As for my thoughts on the project—I liked the idea of it, and loved the challenge of finding a place for each project, and vice versa, in my poem. I have worked very little in formal verse, but over the last few years have devised my own one-poem forms or projects to give myself Frost's 'net.' In my play with form, I have focused on stanza length, syllabics, and reoccurring words or images. One of the things I liked about 'The Twenty Little Poetry Projects' is that the scope of projects was must broader, and not limited to 'poetic' devices, e.g. contradiction, a word never encountered in a poem, nicknames."

Erin O'Keeffe: "I was introduced to this exercise in Terry Wolverton's Basics of Poetry class and I have been an ardent fan ever since. The structure of the exercise, the rules and directions, inspire in me an oddly rebellious sense of freedom and abandon. When I am writing a poem in this form, I become a risky zealot, baring it all in a garish, honest light—a full-tilt boogie. 'Love is' was inspired when I stuck my head under the gleaming hood of a '38 Buick at Bob's Big Boy on Car Night Friday."

Ashlee Owens is a twelve-year-old seventh-grader at Charles Hart Middle School in Washington, D.C. She has been writing since the fourth grade, and would one day like to write a book. In addition to her literary efforts, Ashlee enjoys drawing, cooking, and sports, particularly basketball and tennis. For the past year, Ashlee has been involved in activities with the D.C. Creative Writing Workshop, which provides literary arts programs to at-risk youth in the historically neglected Congress Heights neighborhood. Ashlee received this assignment in her after-school Writing Club, and took it home to work on, "Because I knew I could do it."

Carla Panciera lives in Rowley, MA, with her husband and three daughters. Her work has appeared in several publications, including *Nimrod*, *The Chattahoochee Review*, *The Sycamore Review*, and *Kalliope*. Her poetry has been nominated for a Pushcart Prize.

"I write every day and there are only so many muses to go around. Therefore, I was excited to have a creative prompt to work from. The exercises encouraged me not to take myself so seriously—good advice for poets. Once I read the foreign phrase requirement, I thought of my disastrous trip to Paris. It was great to remember all the laughs that went along with our misadventures."

Jackie Petto is a Creative Writing major at Western Michigan University. She is a "beginner" whose work has appeared in her hometown and in *Voice*. She enjoyed "The Twenty Little Poetry Projects" exercise as it opened her mind to new techniques that, to her naive surprise, weren't restrictive. She is now more conscious of the way she structures poetry and often uses some of the suggestions given in the exercise. Instead of waiting for poems to find her, she now finds them!

Patrice Pinette: "I live in Southern New Hampshire with my husband and two children. I work at a Waldorf High School where I teach creative writing and eurythmy, an art of movement which brings poetry into the realm of dance. (Eurythmy has been called a whirling alphabet in space!)

"In working with 'The Twenty Little Poetry Projects' language itself becomes a gateway to content, be it memory or fantasy. The twists and turns of words in new relations to each other take us down paths we may never have traveled. This is how the poem 'Sundays' came to be written. That arbitrary opening metaphor prompted memories I had never written about. The form of the exercise gave me language for those colorful and awkward impressions from my childhood. The challenge of these poetry projects is of course not only to generate marvelous images, which my students do, but also to find and sustain a unity that links the projects, shaping a poem of integrity as well as one of surprises."

Norine Radaikin, MA in creative writing, CSU Sacramento. Chapbook *Generation* (Poet's Corner Press). Poems forthcoming in *Bardsong Press Anthology*, *Rattlesnake Review*, and *Best of 2000-2004 Anthology*. Previously published in *Sacramento Anthology*, *Tule Review*, *Poetry Now*, *Susurrus*, *Switched-On-Gutenberg*, and others.

"The poem 'Child of Science' is based on a card picked at random from The William Blake Tarot deck (Ed Buryn). The suit of science corresponds to the suit of swords in the conventional tarot. The picture on the card is from a William Blake engraving."

Charles Rammelkamp: Five published poetry chapbooks, *i don't think god's that cruel*, *Go to Hell*, *A Convert's Tale*, *Fire Drill!* and *All Hallow's Eve*, as well as a collection of short fiction, *A Better Tomorrow* and co-editor of a Red Hen Press essay collection, *Fake-City Syndrome*.

"'The Twenty Little Poetry Projects' is a wonderful entry into the joys and imaginative possibilities of poetry. Each exercise uniquely challenges your imagination, but you must still exert creative control over the entire work to present a cohesive whole. I usually start with an image, a story or an idea, but word-for-word and line-for-line the poetic confrontation with language this exercise poses is the same."

Diane Raptosh: "I have published two collections of poetry, *Just West of Now* (Guernica: 1992) and *Labor Songs* (Guernica: 1999). I teach English at Albertson College.

"Just for the heck of it, I tried working with 'The Twenty Little Poetry Projects,' because I grew tired of my usual writing practices. The projects allowed me to relinquish what sometimes feels like the very grave responsibility of writing poetry myself. In the best moments I felt as if I was taking dictation from God. I wrote about twenty such poems and intend to write more."

R. Flowers Rivera is a Mississippi native with a MA from Hollins University and a Ph.D. from Binghamton University. She will be included in *New Sister Voices: Black Women Poets Since 1954*, edited by Allison Joseph. She is a two-time nominee for Pushcart Prize XXVII, and she was a 2001 finalist for the Journal Award in Poetry, the May Swenson Award in Poetry, and the Naomi Long Madgett Award in Poetry.

This newly transplanted Memphian says, "As with the best of forms, these projects ask discipline of the writer to match both stray and focused thoughts with seemingly random requests; and as with most forms, the poet is either immediately delighted or left trying to pinpoint what she's done to make the poem go quite horribly awry. This says nothing of the poet's successive attempts to 'repair' one phrase or a whole slew of lines; she must always be vigilant in assessing the collateral damage—which, in some cases, might be the poem itself." View more of her work by visiting www.promethea.com.

Lee Rossi's poems have appeared in *The Sun, Chelsea, Poetry East, Nimrod, the Apalachee Quarterly*, and many others. His second book of poems, *Ghost Diary*, appeared last year from Terrapin Press. A computer programmer displaced by the caprice and mischief of 9/11, he recently served as birth coach during the delivery of his second child, a daughter named Evelyn.

He writes, "For some time now I've been reading and imitating younger writers like Tony Hoagland, Mark Halliday, and Dean Young, who delight in shredding the mask of sincerity which controls and inhibits so much contemporary poetry. 'The Vulture Knows' was just a more extreme example of the sincere insincerity I'd already been practicing."

Kathleen Anne Roxby, a native of California, was Associate Editor for *Poetry Forum* and currently hosts a monthly poetry reading at her local Borders bookstore. Recent poems appeared in *Art/Life, PMS, Poetry Zone Poets of Santa Barbara, Eternal Portraits,* and *Letters from the Soul.* She has three chapbooks, *Chameleon Woman, Paperdoll* and *Tangent/Allusion.*

"Poem's evolution. Number 1: Looking for inspiration outside my window, I saw a wind-whipped tree shaped like an Irish harp. Number 2: Tree monkeys suggested Asia which led to Thailand for Number 5. Having visited Thailand during the Viet Nam War triggered several war images. Number 14 returned me to my desk. Number 18: Sad tree gets a sad Jacques Brel song lyric.

"I thoroughly enjoyed the challenge of 'The Twenty Little Poetry Projects' exercise and have shared it with my poet friends. One group of poets who regularly present poetry readings at the local Borders Bookstore plan to use the exercise for scheduled on-site writing exercises in the coming months. The three poems that I wrote are not anything that I would have otherwise written. That in itself was a revelation. Since then, I have written another poem, 'The Ain't Nobody Tag,' which was entirely inspired by number 8."

Lynn Schmeidler is a writer, teacher, and educational consultatnt. Her prose and poetry have most recently appeared in *River City, Full Circle Journal, Room of One's Own,* and Lonely Planet's *Rite of Passage.* Lynn leads creative writing workshops from her home in Dobbs Ferry, NY.

"I wrote 'My Muses Sit Upon Uncomfortable Chairs' in a sort of lucid dream state—the rational side of my brain checked off each of 'The Twenty Little Poetry Projects' as it was completed, while my unconscious repeatedly called up connections that surprised me. Actually writing the poem upstairs with children and sitter below, the exercise was the babysitter of my mind—focusing and playing with my thoughts."

Pearl Stein Selinsky: Master's in Creative Writing. First place in both the *Bazzanella* and *Room Of One's Own* competitions sponsored by the English department at the California State University, Sacramento. Have taken a number of prizes in poetry competitions. Served as judge in poetry competitions, and gave an invitational reading at California State University, Sacramento as part of the annual arts festival in April, 2000. Published in *Vintage 45*, in anthologies: *Only In Her Shoes*, and *To Honor A Teacher*, and the magazines: *Poetry* (Chicago), *Ekphrasis, Poetry Now, Tule Review, P.D.Q., 33 Review, The Prairie Star, Mediphors*, among others.

"By coincidence, this exercise was introduced to me during a workshop the week before the call for poems in response to it. I polished the results of my workshop effort to submit to Writers At Work; a very interesting aspect of this piece is that I am an only child, one who has always yearned for a sibling."

Evie Shockley's poetry appears in her chapbook, *The Gorgon Goddess* (Carolina Wren Press: 2001) and in print and online publications including *Ashville Poetry Review, Beloit Poetry Journal, "Bessie, Bop, or Bach:" An Anthology of Poems from the Diversity in African American Poetry Festival* (forthcoming), *Crab Orchard Review, Hambone, HOW2, nocturnes (re)view of the literary arts, Oyster Boy Review, Poetry 180: A Turning Back to Poetry, Poetry Daily: Poems from the World's Most Popular Poetry Website*, and *Titanic Operas*. Shockley, a graduate fellow of Cave Canem and member of the Carolina African American Writers Collective, teaches literature at Wake Forest University.

Ann Silsbee was a composer, with works performed and recorded in the USA and abroad. Her poems have appeared in the *Seneca Review, Atlanta Review, Spoon River Poetry Review* and many others, and in a chapbook, *Naming the Disappeared*. Her book, *Orioling*, won the 2002 Benjamin Saltman Prize and was published by Red Hen Press. Ann passed away in 2003.

"'The Twenty Little Poetry Projects:' a bit like following clues on a treasure map, discovering one by one solutions to each, with no idea where the clues were leading. The demand to fulfill the conditions freed the mind to rove in quite unexpected directions."

Anne Silver is author of *Bare Root: A Poet's Journey with Breast Cancer* (Terrapin Press: 2002). A poet since 1968, Anne holds two Masters Degrees—in poetry and psychology—and has been an expert handwriting witness. She resides in Los Angeles and is one of the 2004 winners of the Passenger contest. Her book, *Instant People Reading*: Career Press, has been in print since 1984. She has been published in *Atlanta Review, University of Miami Press, Nimrod, Red Wheelbarrow, Hurricane Alice, Green Hills Literary Lantern, 88, Southern Humanities Review, Westview, Daybreak, Spoon River, Bridges, California Quarterly, Libido, Shelagh Na Gig,* and *Birmingham Review.* Her work will appear in *Death, Be Not Proud,* an anthology with four U.S. poet laureates.

Jim Simmerman is the author of four books of poetry, *Home* (chosen by Raymond Carver as a Pushcart "Writer's Choice" selection), *Once Out of Nature* (a "Best of the Small Presses" Book Exhibit selection at the Frankfurt Book Fair), *Moon Go Away, I Don't Love You No More* (nominated for the Pulitzer Prize and the National Book Award), and *Kingdom Come*; and is co-editor of the anthology *Dog Music: Poetry About Dogs.* The recipient of a Pushcart Prize and fellowships from the NEA, the Arizona Commission on the Arts, the Provincetown Fine Arts Work Center, and others, he is Professor of English at Northern Arizona University.

Renee Simms: "I write primarily poetry but on good days I write fiction, on bad days: creative non-fiction, and each day I scribble unreadable Grocery Lists or To Do Lists or What I Forgot To Do Lists. My writing (not including the lists) has appeared online, in magazines and in various anthologies.

"I enjoyed writing 'The Death of Soul' using 'The Twenty Little Poetry Projects' exercise. I'd been trying to write a poem about growing up in Post-Motown Detroit. The exercise helped to contain this rather large topic and it caused me to embrace humor which greatly improved the poem."

David Starkey teaches in the MFA program at Antioch University-Los Angeles, and is the author of a textbook, *Poetry Writing: Theme and Variations* (NTC: 1999), as well as several collections of poems from small presses, most recently *Fear of Everything*, winner of Palanquin Press's Spring 2000 chapbook contest, and *David Starkey's Greatest Hits* (Pudding House: 2002). In addition, over the past fourteen years he has published more than 300 poems in literary magazines such as *American Scholar, Beloit Poetry Journal, Cutbank, High Plains Literary Review, The Journal, Massachusetts Review, Mid-American Review, Notre Dame Review, Poet Lore, Sycamore Review,* and *Wormwood Review.*

Melissa Stein's poems have appeared in *American Poetry Review, Many Mountains Moving, North American Review, Crab Orchard Review, Seneca Review, River City, Calyx,* and many other journals, and anthologies. She is a freelance writer and editor in San Francisco.

"'The Twenty Little Poetry Projects' exercise has generated some of my quirkiest and most offbeat poems, and some of the poems I've most delighted in writing/revising. Like many poetic forms with 'rules,' I never know where this exercise will take me—which is probably why I keep coming back to it! The italicized lines in the first stanza are a reference to Nina Cassian's poem 'Temptation.'"

Michael Bernard Sykes: "This year I will be forty. I am a stand up comedian and a musician who is completing his final enlistment in the military. Writing has always been an accidental venture for me. I usually write when I find myself bound in silence and solitude. It wasn't until I met Cheryl Floyd-Miller and joined MonkeyBREAD four years ago that I started writing with any focus. This is my only submission in four years of writing. This poem was written two years ago.

"This poem was born of an exercise that I found to be a challenge. It took me completely out of my game since I have a very lyrical sense when it comes to writing. I use musical rhythms to establish my meter. I was forced to dissect the poem line by line. I wrestled with it. I was worried that one line would not connect to the next. It wasn't until I decided not to fight the exercise that the poem was finally born. I really liked the exercise and the result. I may write a whole series of poems based on the format. After I was finished, I was like 'Whoa! Check me out!'"

Susan Terris' book *Natural Defenses* has just been published by Marsh Hawk Press and a letter press edition of her book *Poetic License* will also be published in 2004. *Fire is Favorable to the Dreamer*, was published by Arctos Press in 2003. It has been named "Best Poetry Book of 2003" by the Bay Area Independent Publishers Association. Other recent books of poetry are: *Curved Space* (La Jolla Poets Press: 1998), *Eye of the Holocaust* (Arctos Press: 1999) and *Angels of Bataan* (Pudding House Publications: 1999). Recent fiction: *Nell's Quilt* (Farrar, Straus & Giroux). Her journal publications include *The Antioch Review, The Midwest Quarterly, Ploughshares, Calyx, Shenandoah, Hunger Mountain, Hotel Amerika, Missouri Review,* and *Southern California Anthology.* With CB Follett, she is co-editor of a new journal, *RUNES, A Review Of Poetry.* In the last four years she has had sixteen different poems nominated for Pushcart Awards. She is the 2003 winner of the George Bogin Award offered by the Poetry Society of America.

"How did it feel to write it? 'The Twenty Little Poetry Projects' made me feel free. I felt like I was flying when I wrote it, like I had permission to do or say anything!"

Susan Thomas: "My collection, *State of Blessed Gluttony* (Red Hen Press: 2004) won the Benjamin Saltman Prize. I also have a chapbook, *The Hand Waves Goodbye,* published by Main Street Rag in 2002. I was recipient of the 2003 Iowa Award for Poetry and the recipient of the 2003 Ann Stanford Prize.

"It was fun doing this exercise because the strategy of the poem-to-be was already provided. Associations could head off, (capriciously), in one direction, but there was always the subversion (and mischief) of the next project around the bend in case I was getting bored."

Lynne Thompson's work has appeared or is forthcoming in *Poetry International, Indiana Review, Crab Orchard Review, Runes, Poetry Daily*, and other journals.

"As a lyric poet who mines 'transparently logical structures,' 'The Twenty Little Poetry Projects' completely threw me! It seemed like a disjointed approach to capturing dreams in 'poem-light and whole.' But once the first line appeared (don't ask me how!), the rest just seemed to flow. I felt as though I'd taken on the perspective of dogs who are perpetually subject to the caprice of humans. I dedicate the poem to them."

Madeline Tiger: "b.1934 in NYC, I've lived in NJ for most of my life. I've been a writer for 61 years, a teacher since 1957, and a grandmother since 1992. My eighth collection of poems is *Birds of Sorrow and Jow: New and Selected Poems, 1970-2000*: Marsh Hawk Press: 2000. I work for NJSCA (WITS) and the Dodge Foundation Poetry Programs. I raised my five kids in Montclair. Now I live in a little house in Bloomfield under a weeping cherry tree.

"I had just returned from a strenuous visit to friends in Haiti when the *Mischief* call appeared on my e-mail. Bleary, I went to Chicago soon after, and plunged into family—carrying K'NEX building puzzles, Calico Critters and 'The Twenty Little Poetry Projects.' They seemed no more disjunctive than 'real' life. The assignment demanded focus, language play, and arrangements that I had to invent. I calmed down to the task in the middle of the family whirligig. This kind of writing requires obedience, a tussle, disobedience, a connecting flow, opening out, and pressing stuff together. (Sounds like potting, doesn't it? or family life!)

"The projects' demands were irritants, then catalysts. Once the word-play entranced me, I stopped attending to 'sense' or narrative. My raw Haitian impressions were triggered to fall into the lines. What a relief to find a place for the clutter of fragments I was carrying. The words engendered more words. They gathered steam, pulling along motifs and themes. I designed a stanzaic form, out of necessity, with all that wild array to gather into some kind of control. Then I had to make sure the skeleton fit the closet. I was motivated to revise endlessly before I let the piece go, and that patience-at-work is a bonus for me.

"Meanwhile, I 'persuaded' my grandson Solomon, then 7, to do it too. Sometimes dragging, he did finish. His winning entry into the anthology was 'poetic justice'—more thrilling for me than managing the crazy work myself."

A.K.Toney is a poet, writer, and performance artist. He is a member of the renowned World Stage Anansi Writer's Workshop in Leimert Park, Los Angeles' cutting edge African American Arts enclave. Toney is also a member of the Hittite Empire, the critically acclaimed African American male performance art group since 1993. He is a co-founding member and principal in the performance art group Ibeji Players. They have performed in L.A. and have lectured at the California Institute of the Arts.

Toney has also performed at the Museum of Contemporary Art as a part of the 1998 Summer Jazz Series; the Los Angeles County Museum of Art as part of the 1998 Harlem Renaissance Exhibit; the J. Paul Getty Center for the Portrait Study Exhibit entitled "what soul eyes have seen," by Curator Michael Datcher; and at the Los Angeles historic Central Library in the Mark Taper Auditorium; Co-Curator of the World Beyond Festival of Poetry sponsored by the World

Stage Performance Gallery and Beyond Baroque Literary Arts Center. He was a recipient of the 2000 Pen USA West Center Emerging Voices Fellowship.

A.K. describes his process as a moment that can be transcribed from or through the medium of truth. There is no matter what form, style, word, voice, sound, light, or language when used. Language being the least in the category, is the "what" when describing a special observance. "Usually when we write, we think what to write, rather than being the moment that is documenting itself."

William Trowbridge's books are *Flickers, O Paradise, Enter Dark Stranger* (U. of Arkansas Press: 2000, 1995, l989), and the chapbooks *The Four Seasons* (Red Dragonfly Press: 2001), and *The Book of Kong* (Iowa State U. Press: l986). His poems have also appeared or are forthcoming in *The Gettysburg Review, Poetry, Boulevard, Epoch, The Georgia Review*, and many others. He is an associate editor of *The Laurel Review*.

"'The Twenty Little Poetry Projects' takes writers into an eerie forest of disorder, fluidity, and potential goofiness where they have to discover the poem while composing it. All but the terminally organized will find the trolls friendly and the treasure abundant."

Kathrine Varnes is editor with Annie Finch of *An Exaltation of Forms: Contemporary Poets Celebrate the Diversity of Their Art* (University of Michigan Press, 2002). Her poems and essays have appeared recently in *Black Warrior Review, Lyric Poetry Review,* and *Valparaiso Poetry Review*. A book, *The Paragon*, will be published by World Tech Press in January 2005. She teaches at the University of Missouri at Columbia.

"'The Twenty Little Poetry Projects' attracted me after I'd been working for several years on an absurdly long narrative crown of sonnets. Adherence to storyline in addition to rhymes and refrains felt like a favorite pair of heels that permanently shortened my Achilles tendon. It feels great to stretch out again."

Pat Viera was born in Havana, Cuba and emigrated to the United States with her family at the age of 9. She has traveled extensively and now makes her home in Los Angeles, where she has been a member of The Women's Poetry Project for almost ten years. Her work is published in *Catena* (Silverton Books) and in *Poetry is Not a Luxury*, an anthology due out in the winter of 2004.

"I knew that to write 'Vanilla is an Orchid' based on 'The Twenty Little Poetry Projects,' I would have to alter my typical writing routine. On an early Saturday morning in the winter of 2002, I drove ninety miles north of Los Angeles and checked myself into a quiet, little hotel in Santa Barbara, California. Surrounded by lush Queen Palms and a glorious view of the sea above bougainvillea draped, Spanish tiled roofs, I decided I would not leave the room all weekend (not even for meals) until I had a solid, working draft of the poem. It was a Hemmingway moment; fog horns through the mist, my hunger, the rain, and finally, satisfaction that I was onto something. I had no pre-conceived idea or intention for the poem but I knew one thing, I wanted to use the line, 'dark skinned slaves accustomed to bitterness who would rather die than cut cane from these chartreuse fields.' I felt this was a powerful, romantic statement with rhythm and stature.

"The process was comedic more than poetic. I would pace around the room with the list of twenty projects and curse at the structure and swear this was not poetry but construction work. It was scandalous, I thought. In the end, after several edits and adjustments, I suppose I could say the poem is part risk, part autobiography, but mostly it was a hell of a lot of fun to write."

Alicia Vogl Sáenz lives in Los Angeles and is of Ecuadorian and Czechoslovakian descent. Her recent publications include: *Poets & Writers, Blue Mesa Review, Drum Voices Revue, Role Call,* and *Grand Street* and is the author of the chapbook *The Day I Wore the Red Coat* (VCP Press: 2000).

"Working with 'The Twenty Little Poetry Projects' was a wonderful exploration between form and whimsy. I loved allowing the language to take me where it wanted to go. It was like wandering in a city as a tourist, finding unexpected images and smells. To me this process was about surrender. I will surrender again and again."

Cheryl D. S. Walker is Chief Operating Officer and General Counsel of Citadel Partners, LLC, a real estate development, design and construction management company. Creating the poem for this project stretched Cheryl beyond her typical style to delve into this magical world of mischief and caprice.

Cheryl writes for innertainment and describes her writing as jazzy, bluesy or hip hop depending upon her mood. She is member of the Eugene B. Redmond Writer's Club and her works have been published in *Break Word with the World* (Southern Illinois University–Edwardsville), *Drumvoices Revue* (Southern Illinois University–Edwardsville), *Eyeball Magazine* (First Civilizations, Inc.), *When the Lions Roar* (Washington University), and www.FYAH.com.

Frank X. Walker, multidisciplinary artist, is a native of Danville, KY, and a graduate of the University of Kentucky. He received an MFA from Spalding University. His most recent book is *Buffalo Dance: The Journey of York* (University Press of Kentucky: 2004). He has lectured, conducted workshops, read poetry, and exhibited at over two hundred national conferences and universities. A founding member of the Affrilachian Poets, he is the editor of *Eclipsing a Nappy New Millennium*: Purdue University's Haraka Press and the author of *Affrilachia: a collection of poems* (Old Cover Press: 2000). His poetry has been widely anthologized in numerous collections including *My Brother's Keeper* (Datcher Press), *Spirit and Flame* (Syracuse University Press), and *Role Call: A Generational Anthology of Social and Political Black Literature and Art* (Third World Press).

Pam Ward is a native of Los Angeles and a graphic designer. Her work has appeared in several publications including *Men We Cherish, Catch A Fire, Calyx, Grand Passion, Caffeine,* and *Sonnets At Work*. She has received a California Arts Council Writing Fellowship and a New Letters Award for Poetry. Her self-published chapbook is entitled *Jacked Up*. She recently completed her first novel, *Want Some, Get Some.*

About this project: "What a piece of work! I loved following the instructions, which is so contrary to my break-the-rules-soul. The '*les bon temps a rouller*' line, which means 'let the good times roll,' came after attending this crazy Creole bash where wild folks were screaming it and dancing like mad while others watched with a break-your-heart-sadness. Car wrecks are such great metaphors for our personal lives, this piece pretty much steered itself."

Michael Waters teaches at Salisbury University on the Eastern Shore of Maryland and for the New England College MFA Program. In Spring 2005 he'll be Stadler Writer-in-Residence at Bucknell. Recent books include *Parthenopi: New and Selected Poems* (BOA Editions: 2001) and (with the late A. Poulin, Jr.) *Contemporary American Poetry* (Houghton Mifflin: 2001). He has also edited *A. Poulin, Jr.: Selected Poems* (BOA Editions: 2001) & co-edited (with Robert Hedin) *Perfect in Their Art: Poems on Boxing from Homer to Ali* (Southern Illinois UP: 2003). His six previous books of poetry include *Green Ash, Red Maple, Black Gum* (BOA Editions: 1997), *Bountiful* (1992), *The Burden Lifters* (1989), *Anniversary of the Air* (1985)—these three titles from Carnegie Mellon University Press—and *Not Just Any Death* (BOA Editions: 1979). He has been the recipient of a Fellowship in Creative Writing from the National Endowment for the Arts, several Individual Artist Awards from the Maryland State Arts Council, and three Pushcart Prizes.

M. Gwin Wheatley, a Mississippian by birth, is a writer of poetry, essays, and short fiction. Her series, *Transplants*, was recently published in *Catena*—a collection of serial poems (Silverton Books: 2003), and her poem, "Ode to H," was a runner-up in the Los Angeles Cultural Affairs Department-funded *Sense of Site*, a poetry postcard project.

"The idea for '*En Durango*, scorpions are king' came from an article in the *Los Angeles Times* about real scorpion hunters. For weeks I was haunted by images of bowls of scorpions and disfigured hunters, and thoughts about my relation as a medical consumer to these people and their difficult work. 'The Twenty Little Poetry Projects' allowed me to take this horrific tale and to imagine the why in the world of *los alacraneros*."

Kelley Jean White, MD: "I was born and raised in New Hampshire, have degrees from Dartmouth College and Harvard Medical School, and have been a pediatrician in inner-city Philadelphia for the past twenty years. I write to survive, returning to poetry when I found myself an unwontedly single mother of three after a very difficult divorce a few years ago. I started sending work two years ago with very modest goals (I hoped to have a half dozen poems published by my fiftieth birthday in 2004) but have had somewhat surprising success, with more than 750 poems accepted or published by about one hundred and seventy-five journals including *American Writing, The Café Review, the Chiron Review, Feminist Studies, The Larcom Review, Minnesota Review, Rattle, Whiskey Island Magazine* and *Nimrod*. A book of my "medical" poems, *The Patient Presents*, was published this spring by The People's Press in Baltimore and a chapbook of very different material, *I am going to walk toward the sanctuary*, was published this fall Nepenthe Books/Via Dolorosa Press. I received a Pushcart nomination for an experimental piece (from Gravity Presses) in 2000, my first year of submission. This spring I have received a contract to publish a second chapbook,

Blues: Songs for Desdemona, with Via Dolorosa Press and to publish *At the monkey-feast table* with ZeBook, a new online poetry publisher. My children and I are shocked by this success.

"I've had a great deal of fun with 'The Twenty Little Poetry Projects' since I encountered them in a workshop with Harriet Levin last year at the nearby Manayunk Arts Center. I've been immersing myself in poetry as much as my full-time medical work and family allow; are very useful for me and this one, well, it sends me into unexpected streets and corners every time, I surprise myself, and isn't that what a poet hopes to do? (R. Frost, 'No surprise in the poet, no surprise in the reader.')"

Jill Williams: Originally from Hartford, Connecticut, Jill Williams divides her time between Vancouver, British Columbia, and Sedona, Arizona. Author of a Broadway musical (Rainbow Jones) and four nonfiction books, she has been published in numerous journals and mainstream magazines. She has two poetry books, "The Nature Sonnets" (Gival Press: 2001) and "A Weakness For Men" (Woodley & Watts: 2003). Website: www.jillwilliams.com.

"As a formalist, I like the challenge of rhyming words as well as using fresh images. That's why Jim Simmerman's 'The Twenty Little Poetry Projects' was so appealing to me. I'd been wanting to write a sonnet about manic depression for a long time and his unconventional suggestions seemed a perfect way to go about it."

Katherine Williams, while making transgenic mice at UCLA, has authored four chapbooks and been a featured poet at Beyond Baroque Literary Arts Center, KXLU FM 88.9, and the Valley Contemporary Poets; she has received further encouragement by way of a Pushcart nomination, first prize in a poetry slam, and the Curator's Choice Gala Reading of the Los Angeles Poetry Festival.

"I did not think much about what to write as I undertook the twenty tasks. Halfway through I noticed that some kind of narrative was taking shape, and by the end I realized I had written a meditation on how unique and ephemeral a day is, and how this awareness is more than most of us can usually handle. At its best, my own work speaks to me as freshly as the work of others, having actuated the voice of my unconscious. Tasks like Simmerman's facilitate this process by creating a writing situation in which the left brain does not know what the right brain is doing."

Niama Leslie Williams: "I printed out the call, enticed by the promise of payment. Poets are hungry, always. The instructions seemed impossible; no way I could blend that crazy list into a coherent poem. But I sat down to it one night and the poem came like cream skimmed off the top. The process I had come to count on, my habit of practicing my craft, came to the fore. I am an instructor at the community college level and a doctoral student, but that experience sticks in my mind like a first kiss and the memory remains just as sweet."

Tamar Diana Wilson "I have published poetry in *Blue Mesa Review, Thema, Saturday Afternoon Journal,* and elsewhere, and published short stories *Anthropology & Humanism Quarterly* and in *Struggle,* a left-wing publication. I am an anthropologist, usually resident in Los Cabos, Mexico, occasionally and intermittently at work on a novel about undocumented Mexican immigrants in Los Angeles in the 1980s. I have a number of publications in academic journals, including *Human Organization, Journal of Borderlands Studies, Review of Radical Political Economics, Latin American Perspectives, Violence Against Women, Critique of Anthropology* and *Urban Anthropology*. Recently my first book, called *Subsidizing Capitalism: Brickmakers on the U.S.-Mexican Border,* has been accepted by SUNY press.

"I printed out the instructions for the poetry format and sat down with them beside the window to my terrace with its cactus and bougainvillea and myriad cats. I immediately decided to write about what was most pressuring me at the moment: my possible divorce from a man I had loved deeply but who had become abusive. I followed step by step the instructions, mixing them around to make greater sense! And the experience of writing it was fun and capricious!"

Terry Wolverton is the author of five books: *Embers,* a novel in poems, *Insurgent Muse,* a memoir; *Bailey's Beads,* a novel; and two collections of poetry, *Black Slip* and *Mystery Bruise*. She has edited twelve literary compilations, including the award winning *His: brilliant new fiction by gay men* and *Hers: brilliant new fiction by lesbians.* She is at work on a novel and a new collection of poems.

"'Hermano Grande' was written to recount an expensive phone call from a tiny town in the south of France to an unrequited love in Los Angeles. Many of us Anglos, on that trip to France, found ourselves sputtering in Spanish (a language in which we were also not fluent) in an attempt to grapple with French."

Mitsuye Yamada's recent publication, *Camp Notes and Other Writings,* published by the Rutgers University Press, is a combined edition of her first two books. She is presently Adjunct Associate Professor in Asian American Studies at University of California, Irvine, and founder of the MultiCultural Women Writers. She is a board member of the Interfaith Prisoners of Conscience, an organization that supports political prisoners in the United States as well as an active member of the Committee on International Development of Amnesty International USA which promotes and funds development of human rights work in Third World countries.

"This exercise sent me back to my childhood following instructions, word for word, line by line, not paying any attention to connections or coherence. It was a supreme distraction during the many hours I sat by my husband's bedside, images of death the one overriding presence. Rereading the final product made me realize that nothing in my life is unqualified, absolute, fixed black and white. I'm just a jumble of gray, contradictory, mixed feelings!"